Women Who Met the Master

ENCOUNTERING JESUS IN THE GOSPELS

CAROLYN CULVER

REGULAR BAPTIST
RBP Press

Women Who Met the Master
© 2016 Regular Baptist Press • Arlington Heights, Illinois
www.RegularBaptistPress.org • 1-800-727-4440
Printed in U.S.A. All rights reserved.
RBP5168 • ISBN: 978-1-62940-611-4

Third printing—2022

Contents

Preface

JESUS SET A WONDERFUL EXAMPLE through the love and compassion He showed to women. His interactions with women were quite contrary to the culture of the Jewish people. In the culture of Jesus' day, the rabbis did not speak to women in public, and it was not common for women to be taught religious truth. Rather than being condescending to women like other Jewish men were, Jesus treated them with respect and communicated that He saw them as persons of value and worth. His respectful treatment was revolutionary and reflected His attitudes and actions just as consistently as His other teachings.

The Talmud is a printed collection of ancient Jewish thought. In includes many of the oral traditions of Jesus' day, such as rules and prayers. Through these writings, we are able to gain much insight into the culture. In reciting daily prayers, it was common for Jewish men to speak the following three-fold thanksgiving:

> *Praised be God that he has not created me a gentile; praised be God that created me not a woman; praised be God that he has not created me an ignorant man* (Menahot 43b).

Another Rabbinic teaching asserts:

> *Let the words of the Law (Torah) be burned rather than be committed to a woman ... If a man teaches his daughter the Law, it is as though he taught her lechery* (Sotah 3.4).

Instead of affirming those traditions, Jesus spoke to women publicly, taught women spiritual truth, touched them and permitted them to touch Him, healed them, allowed women to travel with Him, praised their service and faith, accepted their worship, and considered them to be valid witnesses.

Jesus never humiliated nor exploited a woman. He accepted questions and requests seriously and responded without flattery, coaxing, patronizing, joking, or condescension. There is no record in the Gospels of a woman who denied Him, deserted Him, or betrayed Him. According to Matthew, Mark, and Luke, women remained at the cross after the death of Jesus, and all four of the Gospel writers record that women were the first to appear at the tomb after His resurrection.

This study examines each of the occasions recorded by the writers of Matthew, Mark, Luke, and John in which Jesus spoke to a woman or a girl. Each account will be examined in the order that it happened, but when a particular character is referenced in multiple accounts, all of those events will be addressed in the same lesson.

Jesus' Interactions with Women
An Overview

DURING MANY OF THE MORE challenging times in my life, I have wanted to listen to audible words from Jesus, ask questions and receive verbal answers, hear an absolute answer, feel His physical touch of comfort, see His eyes of forgiveness, and even crawl onto His lap and into His embrace for the assurance of His love and care. I have wondered what it must have been like to meet Him on a path, to eat a meal with Him, or to sit at His feet while He taught. In the Gospels, we can read many accounts of His personal encounters and conversations with women, and we have the privilege of listening in, learning from them, and having our lives changed because of His words. His words to women years ago contain messages for us as well.

Personal Recall

1. When you think of women Jesus addressed in the Gospels, who comes to mind?

2. Do you have a favorite story of a woman with whom Jesus personally interacted? If so, who is it?

3. Think about the opportunity to approach Jesus directly as He walked as a man on the earth. What are some of the needs and requests you would expect women to communicate to Him?

Personal Discovery

In each of the following passages, Jesus addresses a woman. As you look at each set of verses, determine to whom Jesus spoke. Then record the words Jesus spoke.

Passage	Setting	Person Addressed	Jesus' Words
Luke 2:41–50	Mary and Joseph had taken Jesus to Jerusalem for the Feast of the Passover. Jesus stayed behind when the family joined others for the return to Nazareth. His parents found Him in the temple.		
John 2:1–11	There was a wedding at Cana in Galilee. The embarrassing situation of the shortage of wine was presented to Jesus, and He performed His first recorded miracle.		
John 19:26, 27	From His physical position on the cross, Jesus saw His mother and John standing nearby.		
John 4:5–42	Jesus departed from social custom and initiated a conversation at a public well with an immoral woman of a different culture. As He allowed her to ask questions, He showed respectful consideration for her and offered her that which she needed most.		

Passage	Setting	Person Addressed	Jesus' Words
Matthew 8:14, 15; Mark 1:29–31; Luke 4:38, 39	After leaving the synagogue, Jesus arrived at the house of two of His disciples. Jesus departed from culturally acceptable behavior after family members appealed to Him on behalf of an ill woman.		The Bible does not record anything said directly to her.
Luke 7:11–17	While traveling with a crowd, Jesus met a large funeral procession on its way out of the city to the burial site.		
Luke 7:36–50	At a dinner given for Jesus at the home of a Pharisee, a woman anointed Jesus' feet. In response to the judgmental Pharisee, Jesus offered a verbal defense.		
Matthew 27:55, 56; Mark 15:40, 41; Luke 8:1–3; 23:49	Jesus allowed some who had been cured of evil spirits and diseases to be disciples who followed Him and supported His ministry financially out of their own means. Some of these women were recognized by name as they watched His crucifixion from a distance.		The Bible does not record anything Jesus said specifically to them, except to the mother of James and John (see below) and to them as a group (see below).
Matthew 9:20–22; Mark 5:26–34; Luke 8:43–48	When Jesus was on His way to the home of a synagogue ruler, a woman touched Him with full confidence that the touch would be accompanied by healing.		
Matthew 9:18, 19, 23–26; Mark 5:21–24, 35–43; Luke 8:41, 42, 49–56	A synagogue ruler approached Jesus and implored Him to heal his daughter. While they were on their way, a messenger communicated that the girl had already died.		

Passage	Setting	Person Addressed	Jesus' Words
Matthew 15:21–28; Mark 7:24–30	When a woman of a different ethnicity begged Jesus for help with her daughter, Jesus' disciples asked Him to ignore her. Instead, He responded to her argument of faith.		
John 8:1–11	A woman was used as bait in a ploy to trap Jesus, but He skillfully dismissed those who accused her.		
Luke 10:38–42	Jesus and His disciples were guests for dinner in the home of two sisters and a brother. One of the sisters prepared the dinner while the other one listened to Jesus' teachings. The hostess appealed to Jesus out of frustration when her sister did not offer help with the meal preparation.		
John 11:1–44	After the death of their brother, Jesus interacted with each of the sisters individually.		
Matthew 26:6–13; Mark 14:3–9; John 12:2–8	While Jesus was a dinner guest, a woman worshiped Him in a way that provoked indignation and objection from His disciples. Jesus' response was countercultural in defending a woman's action before a group of men.		
Luke 11:27, 28	While Jesus was teaching about the work of an evil spirit, a woman called out a blessing in a disruptive way. Instead of ignoring her, Jesus corrected her about the greater and more important thing that will be blessed.		

Passage	Setting	Person Addressed	Jesus' Words
Luke 13:10–17	Jesus healed a woman on the Sabbath, in the synagogue, and in the presence of the synagogue ruler. In doing so, He publicly showed concern and regard for someone whom others probably had shunned for years.		
Matthew 20:20–23; 27:55, 56	A mother entreated Jesus for a personal favor, but she did not understand the ramifications of her request. Her ambitious desire for her sons invoked an explanation of truth about being a servant. She was one of the women who were recognized by name as they watched the crucifixion from a distance.		
Luke 23:28–31	Jesus addressed a small segment of the crowd that was mourning and lamenting Him as they followed Him to execution.		
Luke 8:2	Jesus had cast seven demons out of a woman. She became a disciple of Jesus.		Nothing Jesus said to her is recorded until after the Resurrection (see below).
Mark 15:47; 16:9; John 20:11–18	She observed His place of burial. Jesus made His first post-resurrection appearance to her. Though she initially thought the risen Jesus was a gardener, she recognized Him when He said one word. Jesus then gave her the countercultural license and authority to give the first testimony of His resurrection.		

In studying the accounts of Jesus' interactions with women in the books of Matthew, Mark, Luke, and John (the Gospels), it has been amazing to see the balance between the opportunities Jesus gave to women as well as those He gave to men. As Vickie Kraft and Gwynne Johnson point out in *Women Mentoring Women*, the Bible records songs by both Mary and Zacharias. Both Simeon and Anna welcomed Jesus in the temple. Jesus talked about new birth with the Samaritan woman as well as with Nicodemus. Peter confessed Jesus as "the Christ, the Son of the living God," and Mary of Bethany confessed, "Yes, Lord, I believe that You are the Christ, the Son of God, who is to come into the world." Both a man and a woman were healed in a synagogue. Both a daughter and a son were raised from the dead. Both men and women traveled with Jesus.

Jesus ministered to women as the One Who gave dignity and value to their abilities to think well as students, worship well as believers, and minister well as servants. He did this by speaking to them, teaching them, and commending them. In the gospel accounts, He revealed Himself to women and gave them the opportunity to be changed by Him. Without distinction to gender, Jesus has given every believer the duty and high privilege of learning of Him, believing Him, loving Him, serving Him, and witnessing for Him.

Personal Reflection

4. Have you met Jesus through the pages of Scripture? Have you believed on Him as your Savior? Are you His disciple, learning from and following Him?

5. If you have received Jesus as your Savior, reflect upon some of the ways God has changed you since that time, when your relationship with Jesus Christ began. What are some of the areas in which you know that the changes in you came through listening to Jesus?

6. What a privilege it is to be able to learn of Christ, to believe Him, to love Him, to serve Him, and to witness for Him. Write a prayer that expresses your desire to focus on the privileges He has given you.

Mary, the Mother of Jesus
A Chosen Woman

I CAN'T IMAGINE the surprise, fear, wonder, and amazement that Mary experienced when she learned she was chosen to be the mother of the Messiah. Even more than that, I can't imagine being the mother of Mary and hearing her testimony about an encounter with an angel! We don't know how Mary's family responded to her news, but we wonder what our own response would have been.

Luke records the first interaction between Jesus and a woman; not surprisingly, the woman is His mother. Though Mary was such a significant person to Christ, the Bible gives few details about their relationship or conversations. And, apart from Mary's cousin Elizabeth, no information is given about Mary's family.

The Bible does not record any interaction between Jesus and His mother until Luke 2:41–50, but it is important to study Mary's background and experiences before Jesus' birth, as well as their interactions as mother and son.

Personal Recall

1. How do many people regard Mary?

2. What do you think may have been the most difficult experiences for Mary?

Personal Discovery

Read Luke 1:26–38.

3. (a) What can we learn about Mary from verses 26 and 27?

(b) How did Gabriel address Mary in verses 28–30?

4. What did he tell her?

The phrase "highly favored" literally means "full of grace." God bestowed a special honor on Mary, and she was a special recipient of His grace.

5. According to verses 31–33, what did the angel tell Mary about the One Who would be her Son?

Mary was not surprised that the Messiah was to come, yet she asked the angel a significant question.

6. What surprised Mary? What was it that she really questioned? Write a paraphrase of Mary's question that expresses what you think represents her heart and confusion.

Though Mary did not question the Messiah's coming or the possibility of God's work, she did question the actual procedure or process. *How* could she be the mother?

7. What was Gabriel's response to Mary's question?

In an act of creation, the Holy Spirit would come upon, or overshadow, Mary. This is the same word that is used in Genesis 1:2 ("moved upon") in speaking of the Spirit's hovering over the waters during the creation of the world.

8. What sign was given to Mary (Luke 1:36)?

Luke 1:38 records Mary's words: "Behold the maidservant of the Lord! Let it be to me according to your word." These statements indicate that Mary submitted to God's plan. Perhaps Jesus was conceived at that moment of consent.

Read Luke 1:39–56.

When Mary went to visit Elizabeth at her home, Elizabeth greeted her with a significant statement.

9. (a) What was Elizabeth's greeting?

   (b) What do you see as implications of the things said to Mary in Luke 1:42–45?

Elizabeth's use of the word *blessed* communicates her recognition that Mary had been blessed by God. When she used the preposition indicating "among," she recognized that Mary was not above other women. When she identified Mary as "the mother of my Lord," she expressed her confidence that Mary's Child was the Messiah. Surely, she could not have known this aside from the Holy Spirit's illumination.

10. When Mary praised God for His special favor on her and on Israel, what are some indicators that she recognized herself as a sinner and that she understood her Child to be the fulfillment of covenant promises?

Read Matthew 1:18–25.

An angel told Joseph that Mary's pregnancy was not caused by a man but was a miracle of the Holy Spirit. He had decided to dissolve his betrothal to Mary in a private way, but after the angel intervened, he changed his decision and agreed to name Jesus, an act of legal paternity.

Six months later, Joseph and Mary were still betrothed and traveled more than seventy miles through mountainous terrain to Bethlehem. Mary gave birth to Jesus, wrapped Him in cloths, and laid Him in a manger.

Mary remained a virgin until after Jesus was born. It is important to note that not only was there a virgin conception, but a virgin birth. It is also significant that Mary did not remain a virgin after Jesus' birth: she and Joseph had children together (Matthew 13:55; Acts 1:14; Galatians 1:19).

Read Luke 2:19–34.

In Luke 2:19–34, note some of the things Mary did:
- She pondered things in her heart (Luke 2:19).
- When Jesus was eight days old, she took Him to be circumcised. This was an outward sign of the Abrahamic Covenant, and it showed Jesus to be Jewish (Luke 2:21).
- When Jesus was forty days old, she took Him to the temple in Jerusalem (six miles away) to dedicate Him (Luke 2:22).
- She listened to Simeon's blessing and marveled at the things he said about her child (Luke 2:33).
- She listened to Simeon as he addressed her (Luke 2:34).

11. What was Simeon's message to Mary in verses 34 and 35?

12. As you think of Mary's life, what are some of the sorrows she experienced that were fulfillments of Simeon's prophecy?

The Bible does not recount any event in Jesus' childhood between the ages of forty days and twelve years.

Read Luke 2:41–51.

The dialogue between Jesus and His mother in Luke 2:19–34 is the first recorded. Jesus went with Mary and Joseph to the annual Feast of the Passover (probably for the first time) when He was twelve years old. His parents started their return trip to Nazareth in a very large caravan. At the end of the day's travel, Mary and Joseph realized that Jesus was not with their group, so they traveled back to Jerusalem the following day and then spent part of the next day searching for Him.

13. (a) Where did Mary and Joseph find Jesus?

(b) What was He doing?

In words of exasperation mixed with relief, Mary rebuked her Son for staying behind, but Jesus asked why she and Joseph didn't know that He had to be in His Father's house.

14. What did Jesus' response to Mary communicate about Him and His relationship with His mother?

Jesus was submissive and obedient to Mary in leaving the temple when she rebuked Him, but His question about why they had been searching for Him was an acknowledgment of the reason He had come to earth and the mission He had been given. He was clearly cognizant of His true Father and His mission.

Read John 2:1–11.

The next time an interaction with Mary is recorded is in John

2. Mary was already at a wedding feast in Cana of Galilee before Jesus and several disciples arrived to attend it as well. Mary's role at this event prompts curiosity as well as the revelation of Jesus as the Messiah. When the host, who was probably a close friend or relative of Mary's, ran out of wine, Mary turned to Jesus to solve the problem. Have you ever wondered what Mary might have expected Him to do? According to John 2:11, Jesus had not performed a miracle prior to this, so we don't see that Mary had any reason to expect Him to do so at this point.

Jesus' response to Mary may sound strange, but "woman" was a polite, kind term. "What does your concern have to do with Me" sounds harsh, but it was a common phrase that established a boundary in their relationship. Jesus did not answer His mother with disrespect; but through His answer, He communicated to her that He had moved from dependence upon her personal authority. He declared that the governing will of His life had shifted from her to His Father.

James M. Howard suggests that Mary's expectation of Jesus models a demonstration of true faith. Howard says that Mary is the first person in the Gospel of John to manifest trust in Jesus' words.[1]

15. How did this experience demonstrate Mary's belief in
    Jesus' deity?

In this interaction between Jesus and Mary, Jesus implied that from this point, His actions would be in accord with His own will and that of God the Father. He communicated that the period of His subjection to earthly parents had ended and His work as Messiah had begun: He was on a different timetable and under a different authority.

Mary's instructions to the servants are her last recorded words. Through them, she stepped aside, communicating to the servants that they were to turn from her to Jesus. She clearly commanded action based solely on the word of her Son.

Read John 19:26 and 27.

Just before His death on the cross, Jesus spoke to His disciple John about His mother. In these verses, Jesus showed significant care and honor for Mary when He specifically committed her into John's care and asked John to regard her as his own mother.

16. How did Simeon's prophecy become a personal reality for Mary at the cross?

Mary, the mother of Jesus, has been misrepresented by those who teach that she was sinless and remained a virgin throughout her life. Consequently, many believers have spoken little of her and may have failed to see her courage and hope. They may have minimized her desire to witness for the glory of her Son. May we, like Mary, make Christ known, witnessing for His glory and showing hope and courage in the assignments He gives.

Personal Reflection

17. As you reflect upon Mary's words in Luke 1:38 and 46–55 and consider your own degree of willingness to be used by God, can you truly call yourself His servant? Why or why not? What area of your thinking needs to be adjusted in order for you to experience greater commitment to anything God asks of you?

18. Write a prayer of praise and response to God in which you express submission to Him as His servant. Paraphrase "let it be to me according to your word" (Luke 1:38) in a way that makes a commitment of your own life.

19. Based upon these accounts from the Bible, what is the message Mary would want to proclaim to women today? What would she want us to know about Jesus? What would she want us to know about herself?

Endnote

1 James M. Howard, "The Significance of Minor Characters in the Gospel of John," *Bibliotheca Sacra* 163 (January 2006): 649.

The Woman of Samaria
An Unfulfilled Woman

OVER THE YEARS, I have practiced a variety of approaches toward unbelievers in an effort to bridge the gap between us so I could share my faith in Jesus Christ. I have looked for common interests or training, a common phase of life, and common family situations. I have looked for ways to meet others' needs. I have established relationships based on a foundation that I hope will allow me the privilege of speaking truth. Perhaps you have wanted to share with someone the good news about Jesus—the salvation that He has made available to all people—but you felt that the two of you didn't have anything in common.

Jesus had nothing at all in common with the woman He talked to in John 4. A Jewish man talking to a Samaritan woman . . . the perfect Man interacting with a woman of poor reputation . . . the Giver of life reaching out to a thirsty, unfulfilled woman. Already I am convicted as I recognize that Jesus had nothing in common with me either. My discomfort increases as I think of the people I avoid—the ones I don't speak to about Christ because we don't have any common ground.

Jesus, the master of communication and teaching, had many meaningful conversations and was always able to use piercing questions to turn those dialogues into heartfelt lessons. The longest recorded conversation Jesus had with anyone was with a woman whose name is unknown.

Personal Recall

1. Before reading the account of Jesus' conversation with "the woman at the well," what are the facts you already know about her?

Think of some women within your sphere of influence who struggle in a similar situation. Search your heart about how inclined you are to approach them with a loving and accurate presentation of salvation.

2. What are the first names of two women in your life whose lifestyles evidence dissatisfaction and lack of fulfillment?

Personal Discovery

Read John 4:5–42.

John 4:5–42 records the dialogue Jesus had with a woman at a well. She is identified as "a woman of Samaria." He even calls herself "a Samaritan woman." Otherwise, this passage refers to her eight more times simply as "the woman."

3. What does the passage communicate about her reputation, history, and living situation?

Jesus set a wonderful example through the love and compassion He showed to women in general. As we identify the woman of Samaria's lifestyle, we must marvel at Jesus' personal and respectful interaction with her. Rather than being condescending to all women as other Jewish men were, Jesus communicated to this immoral woman that He saw her as a person of value and worth.

Jesus was completely aware of her history and current living situation, but He departed from all social customs and talked with her alone. He surprised her by treating her as someone worth His time, kindness, and offer of living water of eternal life. Very soon into the conversation, Jesus began a profound discussion of theology as He talked to her about what matters most.

If you are able to access the *Gospel of John* film, please watch the video clip of this account. This film is available on DVD in many libraries, and the interaction can be viewed on YouTube at www.youtube.com/watch?v=6bt_9NZe-E4.

While watching this interaction, try to picture how this woman must have felt as Jesus talked to her.

  4. Notice what Jesus communicated to her. What observation can you make about the way Jesus directed this conversation?

Jesus' interaction with this woman took place at a public well near the town of Sychar, part of Samaria. It was a deep well, one fed by a spring, one with very good water. It was about noon when Jesus sat down to rest at the well. A woman came to perform the daily task of drawing water. Socially, this individual had three strikes against her—she was a woman, an immoral one, and a Samaritan.

The hostilities between Jews and Samaritans went as far back as when wicked King Omri built a temple and an altar to Baal and named the surroundings Samaria. Marriages took place between Israelites and Samaritans, and these families became idol worshipers. Years later, after the Jews were released from Babylonian captivity and began to rebuild the temple and Jerusalem, the Samaritans offered to help. Their help was refused, so they built their own temple on Mount Gerizim and proclaimed it as the only right place to worship. They professed to believe in God, waited for the Messiah, and took pride in claiming Jacob as their forefather.

Though Jesus was God as well as a perfect male Jew who had nothing in common with this Samaritan woman, He spoke gently and set aside all cultural barriers in order to get her attention.

5. What are some of the key elements Jesus used in this conversation?

6. What was the Samaritan woman's greatest need?

Jesus asked the woman to give Him a drink, and then He showed her that she was the one in need of water. At first, she thought He was talking about the liquid water she had come to draw. She knew that she, like all of us, had a need for physical water. It has been said that of all the physical wants a person can feel, none is more intense than the want of water.

The woman of Samaria needed something that would permanently quench the thirst and emptiness of her life. Jesus offered her something that was far greater than what she could give Him: salvation through spiritual water. But she didn't know it right away.

Jesus did not answer her questions directly or get caught in a debate, but He moved to the issues that were most important. He addressed the greatest need in her life. She didn't recognize Who He was, and she didn't understand His meaning, but He shared it anyway. She did understand that He was offering her something better, something that would not require a daily trip to the well.

Read John 4:13–15.

7. What are some of the characteristics of this water Jesus was talking about?

Jesus told the woman that the water He was offering was a gift and that the person who drank it would never thirst again. Our soul are never satisfied if all we have is only physical. But we will be satisfied if we have a spring, a fountain, or a cistern inside of us, where the supply never ends because the source of our satisfaction is Jesus Christ.

When the woman expressed her desire for the water Jesus was offering, He wanted her to understand more fully, so He pointed out a deeper level of need.

Read John 4:16–19.

8. What instruction did Jesus give the woman?

9. How did the woman respond to Jesus' knowledge of her life?

Read John 4:20–24.

When the Samaritan woman changed the subject to the proper place of worship, perhaps she actually had a different question. It seems that she really wanted to know the difference between the faith of the Samaritans and the faith of the Jews, because she had been taught that the place really did matter.

10. Rather than affirming the importance of the place of worship, what response did Jesus give her, and where did He direct her focus?

While it is true that our worship of God can take place anywhere, we should be certain that it is in spirit and in truth. Our worship should be through the ministry of the Holy Spirit and according to the truth that has been given to us in God's Word.

Read John 4:25 and 26.

When the woman told Jesus that she was waiting for the Messiah, Who would reveal the truth about true worship, Jesus identified Himself as the Messiah. He helped her get to the point where she understood that she was a sinner in need of salvation, that her religious system could not save her, and that salvation comes only through faith in Jesus as the promised Messiah.

What a beautiful, life-changing encounter this was! Jesus surprised the Samaritan woman by treating her as someone worth His time, kindness, and offer of living water. When He had finished examining her life, her husbands, the one who was not her husband, her anxiety about where one should worship, and her faith in the Messiah, He gave her His gift of *life*.

Read John 4:28–30 and 39–42.

Jesus' conversation with the woman of Samaria was the first seed in the town of Sychar. John 4:28–30 and 39–42 record the woman's actions after she left Jesus at the well and returned to town.

11. How does this woman model the response of a changed life?

Personal Reflection

The interaction Jesus had with the woman of Samaria is a hopeful account of personal satisfaction. The gift of living water that completely and permanently satisfies is offered to each of us today. Jesus validates every woman as a redeemable person created in the image of God, and He extends an opportunity for satisfaction to all who will accept His gift of cleansing and life.

12. Have you recognized yourself as a sinner, as one who needs spiritual cleansing, and have you received this water of life Jesus was talking about?

13. Jesus communicated to the Samaritan woman that the water He offered to her would be life-changing. Do you remember the first day you took a drink of the water of cleansing, the water of salvation from Jesus? Do you still rely on that water to quench your thirst? Sometimes we can become dissatisfied with what Jesus is offering and what He says to us, and we can start looking for something else to satisfy. In what ways can you give personal testimony to Jesus' claim that the water He offers permanently quenches thirst? Has that been your experience?

14. If you are experiencing thirst and dissatisfaction, go back
    to the water, take another drink, drink it daily, and be satis-
    fied—not with life's situations, but with Jesus Himself. How
    will you do this?

15. Early in His conversation with the Samaritan woman,
    Jesus interacted with her in a profound discussion of theol-
    ogy as He talked to her about what matters most. He took
    time to teach her and to lead her to the point of recogniz-
    ing Him as the Messiah. Jesus demonstrated that His love
    is available to women regardless of past mistakes, hurts,
    pains, and failures. Look back to the beginning of this les-
    son and review the names of women within your sphere
    of influence who are searching for satisfaction. How can
    you demonstrate to them that you really believe the water
    Jesus offers is living and that it gives eternal life?

Peter's Mother-in-Law
and the Widow of Nain
Women of Crisis

I AM GRATEFUL for my daughter-in-law and three sons-in-law. The day each of them joined our family was a wonderful time of celebration, and they have enhanced my life in rich ways. As I study these accounts of Peter's mother-in-law and the widow of Nain, I can't help but think of the changes that happen in families over the years. On the day I became mother-in-law to my children's spouses, we did not contemplate a time when I would need to live with them. We did not project to a time I might be a widow, to a time when they would provide my support, both emotionally and financially.

When we read about Peter's mother-in-law and the widow of Nain, we must understand that so much had happened within the dynamics of their families. Both women experienced great loss and change. It was at this point that Jesus entered their lives.

A mother-in-law and a widow. These two women were not identified by their names, but only by their losses and by a new station of life. Peter's mother-in-law was dependent on her family for housing, and the death of her son caused the widow of Nain to be pitied by her community. Jesus gave attention to both of these women, granting hope and restoring gladness.

Personal serious illness and the death of a child—when these invade a woman's life, they may expend her strength, leave her with few to no answers, and even steal her desire to continue. A woman's serious illness stops the gears of motion within her home, and a loving family is struck by the absence of her service and encouragement. The death of a child cannot be compared to another loss, and it leaves devastating grief that lasts a lifetime.

PART 1
Peter's Mother-in-Law

The healing of Peter's mother-in-law is recorded in the Bible books of Matthew, Mark, and Luke. In each book, only a few verses are dedicated to this account. Nothing the woman may have said is recorded, and her name is not given, yet the event is recorded three different times.

Personal Recall

1. Can you recall a time when you were "touched" by Jesus? While you were experiencing physical illness or emotional exhaustion, did you know that the hand of Jesus caused your hopeless situation to turn to one of healing?

Read Matthew 8:14, 15; Mark 1:29–31; Luke 4:38, 39.

Consider the human writers Matthew, Mark, and Luke. Note the various details that are emphasized by these different writers:

- Matthew addressed a Jewish audience. From his readers' perspective, a Jew who touched a sick person would become unclean.
- In the book of Mark, serving is a sign of greatness.

- Luke was a physician and recorded more specific physical symptoms; the woman's fever had reached a dangerous level.

Personal Discovery

2. (a) Record as many details as you can observe from Matthew 8:14, 15; Mark 1:29–31; Luke 4:38, 39.

(b) Which details are provided by only one of the writers?

3. What information seems to be missing? What are some details that you might expect to be told?

Jesus' compassion was evident. He did not seem to question the request for help, but responded right away. In responding to the need, Jesus departed from culturally acceptable behavior. He was willing to speak to Peter's mother-in-law. He also touched her, a physically ill adult woman, without showing concern for becoming personally unclean.

Much of God's work in our lives occurs because of providence rather than because of miracles. In His providence, God governs all the circumstances of His creation through normal and ordinary events and happenings. On rare occasions, He uses a miracle, a supernatural event that supersedes all natural powers and cannot be explained by physical laws.

This miracle of healing was accomplished within the privacy of a home. Jesus was informed of a need, and He used His supernatural power and divine intervention to heal this woman.

Though God never works contrary to His Word, He is able to supersede all human powers. This happened repeatedly when Jesus lived on earth as a man, and every healing constituted a miracle.

4. Jesus healed the woman's illness. What evidence is given that He went beyond that? In other words, how do we know that He did not just reverse her illness?

This report may not seem significant compared to other healings, but this seemingly lesser account of Jesus' touch on an unnamed woman is a reminder that intercession is never too small or unimportant to Jesus.

Personal Reflection

5. What did you learn about Jesus from this narrative?

6. How do you need the touch of Jesus today? Are you experiencing a need that only He can meet?

7. Who are you praying for today? Are you praying for someone who needs a touch from Jesus on her body, her mind, her marriage, her children?

PART 2
The Widow of Nain

When Jesus met a funeral procession for the only son of a widow from Nain, His heart went out to the mother, and He spoke to her with compassion. His actions were directed toward her son, but He gave a wonderful gift to the woman.

The death of a child, whether as an infant, a child, or an adult, seems to be the greatest grief to endure. This loss is devastating to a parent, changing the future and taking a piece of the parents that cannot ever be replenished. The task of continuing life is daunting, overwhelming, and seemingly impossible.

Personal Recall

8. Think of someone you know who has experienced the death of her child. What were some of the ways she was able to receive help and encouragement?

Do you wonder at the inclusion of this narrative in Scripture? The woman was not named, and we know little about her. There is no reference to her anywhere else in the Bible, yet the Holy Spirit has preserved this record.

Personal Discovery

Read Luke 7:11–17.

9. What emotions does reading this account evoke in you?

Many women are able to identify with, or at least relate to, a similar pain. The raw edge of our own grief helps us to sense the great need and hole in the lives of those who are suffering the loss of a child.

10. What circumstance enhanced this grieving mother's hopelessness?

Jesus and the crowd following Him met the funeral procession at the city gate. The mourners were accompanying the body to its place of burial outside the city, while Jesus was entering the city after traveling from Capernaum.

This widow was weeping as she crossed Jesus' path. We can speculate from the size of the crowd of mourners that she was well respected in her community and was receiving much sympathy, since she had already lost her husband and now suffered the loss of her only son.

As far as we know from Scripture, this woman did not have any prior acquaintance with Jesus, and there is no Biblical documentation that He ever visited the city of Nain again. It appears that Jesus had a divine appointment to meet this woman and to restore life to her as well as to her son.

Consider the culture of Jesus' day. A widow was dependent upon her children, but a widow without children did not have a source of income or means of protection. Not only did this widow have reason for grief, but she was facing a future without hope.

11. (a) What did Jesus say to this widow?

   (b) Jesus stopped the procession and touched the bier. What did He say then?

When Jesus reached out and touched the man's bier, He literally gave the man back to his mother.

12. How would Jesus' act of touching the bier have been perceived by Jewish observers?

Personal Reflection

Jesus overcame the power of death and revealed His awesome power. In restoring physical life to the son, He gave a great gift of renewed life and hope to the mother.

13. What did you learn about Jesus from this account?

14. Has there been a time when you lost all hope and struggled to find a reason for living? If you can, write a prayer of thanksgiving to God for seeing your needs and showing compassion to you by meeting those needs.

15. Do you know someone who is hurting because of great loss? Though you cannot restore what has been lost, how can you show active, involved compassion?

The Woman
Who Anointed Jesus and
the Women Who Followed Him
Women Who Worshiped

PART 1
A Woman of the City Who Anointed Jesus

IN 1984, SONGWRITER Gloria Gaither penned the words to a song that depicts the account preserved in Luke 7:36–50. The first verse and chorus speak of the extravagant display of a woman's love and devotion to Jesus.

One day a plain village woman
Driven by love for her Lord
Recklessly poured out a valuable essence
Disregarding the scorn
And once it was broken and spilled out
A fragrance filled all the room
Like a prisoner released from his shackles
Like a spirit set free from the tomb
Broken and spilled out
Just for love of You, Jesus
My most precious treasure
Lavished on thee

As you begin this lesson, take time to listen to this song. Though it was written by Gloria Gaither, it has been recorded most often by Steve Green and can be heard at www.youtube .com/watch?v=0aHOtPO_lUM.

Personal Recall

1. Which words or lines of the song paint for you a clear picture of this woman's gift?

2. As you reflect upon your own times of personal worship of Jesus Christ, do you recall a time that you gave a gift to Him that others might consider bold or unnecessary?

Personal Discovery

Luke 7 gives an account that is similar to one in the other Gospels, but it is about a different woman. The one in Matthew, Mark, and John will be studied in lesson 9. In both cases, a woman attended a dinner and anointed Jesus with ointment. Observe some of the differences between the two accounts:

The occasion recorded in Luke occurred in Galilee early in Jesus' public ministry. The account given by Matthew, Mark, and John happened much later in Jesus' public ministry, and Jesus announced that the anointing was in preparation for His burial.

The name *Simon* was a common one, but the specific references are very different. The incident in Luke's account occurred at the home of *Simon the Pharisee,* while the other episode took place at the home of *Simon the leper.* In consideration of the Jewish law, it would not be likely for a leper to be an official Pharisee.

In the account written by Matthew, Mark, and John,

Lazarus's sister Martha served the meal, and her sister, Mary, anointed Jesus.

Luke's account does not mention any value or cost of the flask of ointment, but the other three writers indicate that it was valuable.

Luke does not refer to any opposition by Jesus' disciples, but the other three writers quote the disciples' indignant protest.

Read Luke 7:36–50.

Just a short while before this event, Jesus healed Peter's mother-in-law and raised the widow of Nain's son from the dead. Because of this, reports of His miracles had spread and a large crowd of people was following Him. It is likely that the woman in this account observed Jesus while He was in Nain and continued to follow Him.

Luke 7:30 and 36 report that though the Pharisees and lawyers rejected the counsel of God, one Pharisee, Simon, invited Jesus to his house for a meal. Though the Bible does not reveal Simon's motive for the invitation, Luke 7 reveals that Simon did not extend the customary courtesies to Jesus as his guest. There is reason to wonder if Simon was setting a test before Jesus.

The text also does not reveal whether Simon had hired the woman as a servant in his house, or whether she simply arrived without his prior knowledge. It is feasible that she was uninvited yet unchallenged as one of the common guests who were permitted to observe social gatherings. Luke's description of this woman in verse 37 gives specific reason to believe that her reputation was well-known throughout the community. Her name is not given, but her love for the Lord is recorded forever in His Word.

3. How is the woman of this story identified (v. 37)?

There are three characters in this scene: Jesus, Simon the

Pharisee, and the woman. Though Simon the Pharisee was the host and had invited Jesus to his house to eat, he didn't realize that Jesus was Messiah and that He had come to earth to seek and save sinners. Simon did not recognize the importance of showing repentance and was, therefore, surprised that Jesus would associate with a sinful woman. Simon concluded that Jesus did not know the woman's reputation, for surely if He did, He would not have anything to do with her (Luke 7:39). With this assumption Simon demonstrated that he did not perceive Jesus as Messiah.

4. From Luke 7, what can you note about this woman's actions and emotions?

Though Simon did not perceive this woman as a person of worth, her actions of devotion and love certainly surpassed those shown by him. While her attention to Jesus may have seemed extravagant, Simon lacked even customary and expected hospitality.

5. What comparisons did Jesus make between the woman's acts of devotion and love toward Him and Simon's actions toward Him?

This study focuses on Jesus' interaction with the woman, but it would be difficult to overlook the things Simon learned that day after witnessing a sinful woman's devotion and repentance. Jesus responded to Simon's thoughts by telling a story: "There was a certain creditor who had two debtors. One owed five hundred denarii, and the other fifty. And when they had nothing with which to repay, he freely forgave them both." Then He asked Simon, "Tell Me, therefore, which of them will love him more?" Simon answered correctly. He was already well aware of the woman's sinful lifestyle, but on that day, he

admitted to Jesus that lavish forgiveness would result in lavish love, and he heard Jesus' parting announcement to the
woman.

  6. According to the account in Luke, what are the only words
    that Jesus spoke to the woman?

With just a few words, Jesus communicated forgiveness,
salvation, and benediction. After defending the woman to the
judgmental Pharisee, Jesus offered her hope. He announced
that her sins were forgiven.

It is crucial to understand that the woman was saved because
of her faith. Though she loved much and evidenced that love
and devotion to Jesus, she was not forgiven on the basis of that
love. Her guilt caused her grief as she entered Jesus' presence,
and her sobs and tenderness of heart showed her repentance. In
response to being forgiven, she showed great love. What a beautiful picture of faith coupled with appropriate action.

Personal Reflection

The following acrostic can be used when worshiping God
through prayer.

    Adoration of God
    Confession of sin
    Thanksgiving for blessings
    Supplication for concerns

Though none of her words to Jesus are recorded, this woman's actions followed the pattern of ACTS.

    A—She adored Jesus and found a way to show Him her
        adoration.

    C—Probably a prostitute, she knew her sins were many.
        She acknowledged and confessed them with peni-
        tence, grief, and remorse.

T—She poured out her thanks to the only One Who could forgive, cleanse, and change her: the One Who had made her whole.

S—Perhaps she used words in her supplicating for forgiveness. She received forgiveness.

7. Write a personal prayer of worship using the acrostic of **ACTS**.

Go back to the beginning of the lesson and review the lyrics of "Broken and Spilled Out." The last half of the chorus is written below.

> *Broken and spilled out*
> *And poured at Your feet*
> *In sweet abandon*
> *Let me be spilled out*
> *And used up for Thee*

8. What is one sacrificial way you want to be spilled out and used up out of love for Jesus?

PART 2
Women Who Followed and Supported Jesus

Personal Recall

9. Before reading the passage, can you name any female disciples of Jesus?

Personal Discovery

Read Luke 8:1–3.

Several women traveled with Jesus from one town and village to another as He proclaimed the good news of the kingdom of God. In each case, the woman had been cured of evil spirits and diseases and was now a female disciple who followed Jesus and supported His ministry financially out of her own resources (Luke 8:3).

Jesus accepted the support of these women and allowed them to have close and consistent contact with Him. The freedom He gave them by allowing them to travel with Him and participate in His ministry went against their cultural norms.

10. Of the women named in Luke 8:1–3, additional facts are given about two. What do we learn about them?
    • Mary Magdalene

    • Joanna

11. What do their very different stations in life suggest to you about Jesus' followers?

12. (a) In general, to whom could we compare Mary Magdalene today?

    (b) In general, to whom could we compare Joanna today?

    (c) Do you think of such women as sisters in Christ? What is your attitude toward Mary Magdalene? toward Joanna?

13. From Matthew 27:55, 56; Mark 15:40, 41; Luke 8:1–3;
    Luke 24:10, what can be learned about the identity of the
    women who were disciples?

These women served Jesus through their substance and service. Some of them may have been independently wealthy, while others may have made sacrificial donations of money, travel, and hospitality. As they funded the ministry of Jesus and His disciples and as they gave attention to His personal comfort and well-being, they were meeting practical, everyday needs.

These followers of Christ were present when He was crucified. Luke acknowledges the presence of women at the cross, but he does not identify any of them by name. Matthew, Mark, and John all mention Mary Magdalene and another Mary. This other Mary is noted as the wife of Clopas and the mother of the disciple James and his brother Joses. John adds the mother of Jesus, while Matthew and Mark make note of Salome, the wife of Zebedee and the mother of the disciples James and John.

Some of these women followed the body of Jesus to the place of His burial and continued to care for Him by anointing His body with spices. On the morning of the third day, these women returned to the tomb and discovered it was empty. Again, Luke mentions their presence as a group, while Matthew identifies Mary Magdalene and Mary of Clopas. Mark adds Salome, and John mentions only Mary Magdalene. Though the writers don't all name the exact same women, each of them recognizes the women as eyewitnesses who gave Jesus responsible care and grieved for Him at His death. These women were given the privilege of being the first to learn that Jesus' tomb was empty because He had risen from the grave.

Personal Reflection

14. What evidences are there in your life that mark you as a woman who follows Jesus? Can you be considered one of His disciples?

15. Write a prayer thanking God for the women He equips to provide for the needs of His servants.

16. Whether you give out of your poverty or your riches, are you providing money or hospitality to the servants of God, such as missionaries, those on ministry trips, pastors and their families, and so on?

Endnote

1 J. Warner Wallace, "How Many Women Visited the Tomb of Jesus?" http://coldcasechristianity.com/2015/how-many-women-visited-the-tomb-of-jesus.

Personal Reflection

The Bleeding Woman Who Touched Jesus
A Woman Healed through Faith

MANY WOMEN HAVE experienced an extended illness and know that it takes a toll that robs more than physical strength. I have watched strong, successful, serving ladies become discouraged and depressed, hopeless, exhausted, and impatient while trying to navigate a chronic illness. Believing women who have struggled with a debilitating condition that prohibits normal activities know how difficult yet crucial it is to hold on to their faith in God's plan and power. Sickness that extends over a lengthy period threatens to strip stability and perspective and leave weakness, vulnerability, and desperation. What encouragement I have received while watching Christ-following ladies counter these threats by keeping their eyes on Jesus and maintaining faith and hope in Him.

The Gospels of Matthew, Mark, and Luke recount the time a woman who had been bleeding for twelve years risked a great deal and touched Jesus' clothing.

Personal Recall

1. Can you identify and empathize with a woman who has been to multiple doctors and tried various medications and treatments, only to be frustrated and disappointed?

2. How would you try to encourage a woman in this situation?

Personal Discovery

Read Matthew 9:20–22, Mark 5:25–34, and Luke 8:43–48.

Matthew 9:20–22, Mark 5:25–34, and Luke 8:43–48 speak of the same event, but they give different details.

3. What do these passages indicate about this woman's situation?

4. What prompted her to approach Jesus?

Shortly before the interaction between Jesus and this ill woman, He healed the son of a centurion, restored life to the widow of Nain's son, cast demons out of a man from Gadarenes, calmed a stormy sea, and sailed back to Capernaum. He exercised power over nature and demons, and within the hour following this joyous encounter, He demonstrated power over death as He raised Jairus' daughter from the dead. Through the meeting with this bleeding woman, Jesus continued to demonstrate His absolute power that surpasses disease and disability.

According to Mark 3:10 and Luke 6:19, Jesus had healed large crowds of their diseases and evil spirits. Many of these had been healed through touching Him. After being part of a large crowd following Jesus, this desperate woman heard Him speak, saw Him heal others, and became convinced of His power.

5. What do Matthew 9:20; Mark 5:25, 26; and Luke 8:43, 44 disclose about the severity of this woman's bleeding?

Though we do not know her name and though we cannot be certain whether she was a Jew or a Gentile, it is assumed that she was well acquainted with Mosaic law. Under that law, she was ceremonially unclean and prohibited from touching and contaminating anyone. Leviticus 15:25–27 notes specific guidelines for a woman when she had a discharge of blood that extended beyond menstruation.

6. According to Leviticus 15:25–27, what became unclean if the woman touched it?

7. What are some of the social, marital, and spiritual ramifications of this woman's condition?

This woman's bleeding was chronic, though we can only speculate about what might have caused it. Luke, a physician, wrote that the woman had sought help from multiple physicians and still suffered for more than a decade. This seems to confirm that her condition was incurable. In addition to living with a continuing and hopeless disease, she had drained her material resources through her attempts to be healed. When she reached for Jesus, she was experiencing longstanding

illness, poverty, numerous disappointments, and the weariness that accompanies an unresolved trial.

Can you imagine the courage this woman showed simply
by being a part of the crowd? If she had been recognized before she touched Jesus, she might have been treated severely
by others. Since it was necessary for her to live as an outcast—
without the privileges of worshiping in the synagogue, attend-
ing social functions, being involved in compassion ministries,
or pursuing relationships—she showed great courage.

  8. What do Matthew 9:21 and Mark 5:28 indicate about the
     depth of the woman's faith?

After the woman touched Jesus' clothing, Mark 5:29 says
that the source of her bleeding dried up and she was aware of
the change.

  9. What does this point out about the future of her malady?

10. What did Jesus ask the crowd?

Though Jesus did not reveal His purpose for directing those
words to the entire crowd, the Gospels of Mark and Luke record that He was aware of power going out of His body. Since
His power did not depend on anything else, He referred to
His independent ability to work supernaturally, yet He made
choices and governed the use of His power according to His
own will.

11. How did the woman respond to Jesus' question?

This woman continued to show courage and hope. Perhaps
she was tempted to turn around and walk away without being

a spectacle to the crowd. She knew she had been healed, so she had accomplished her goal for that day. Why would she subject herself to the likelihood of humiliation and public ridicule?

It seems that the woman's honesty and gratitude surfaced as she was overcome with the reality of her healing. She also allowed herself to come face-to-face with the One Who had healed her. She had been confident of healing if only she could touch His clothing, and now she responded to His question.

12. What do Mark 5:33 and Luke 8:47 emphasize about her verbal response to Jesus?

13. What were Jesus' parting words to her?

Calling her "Daughter" (Mark 5:34), Jesus spoke to her with the connection of a family relationship and then announced her recovery to the throng of people who had just listened to her confession. The crowd witnessed an unclean woman admit that she had countered the Mosaic law as she touched Jesus intentionally and was healed immediately.

Jesus delivered to her a platform to praise God for His work of healing. He also made a clear statement of the reason for her healing. This believing woman was not healed because of her actions, but because of her faith. Her bleeding did not stop because she had touched Jesus, but because she believed in His power. What a wonderful work Jesus did for this woman! Because of the many people in her own community who were aware of the longevity of her illness, she would not have been able to return to previous activities unless Jesus had restored her. Not only did He heal her of a chronic, incurable disease, but He also changed her from a fearful outcast into a powerful and public witness.

Personal Reflection

14. Reflect upon the times you were simply an observer of
    Jesus and His work in other peoples' lives. Cite at least one
    incident in which you were, metaphorically, not part of the
    curious crowd but actually reached out with longing for a
    personal touch of Jesus' power.

15. In what area of life do you need the personal touch of the
    powerful God? How are you seeking to be close to Him in
    a way that will allow you to experience His work in your
    painful need?

16. According to 2 Corinthians 12:7–10, how can you be victo-
    rious even when God does not grant physical healing?

Jairus' Daughter
A Girl Who Died

THE DEATH OF A CHILD is a life-stopping, unnatural, desperate event. At one point in my husband's pastoral ministry, two children of families in our church died within six weeks of each other. There were no answers, nothing that made sense, little consolation for grieving parents and for a congregation that watched and hurt as well. It was a time to cry out to God, to seek the help and hope that only He could give.

Personal Recall

1. How has God given you opportunity to feel the anguish of parents who plead for the physical life of a child?

2. How has God given you opportunity to rejoice with parents in the unexplainable healing of a child?

Personal Discovery

After Jesus cast demons out of a man and into swine, He got back into a boat and returned to Galilee. A great crowd was waiting for Him and welcomed Him back to their area. One man who was greatly relieved to see Jesus return was Jairus. At the time of his greatest crisis, Jairus waited for Jesus to come back across the sea.

Read Matthew 9:18, 19; Mark 5:21–34; and Luke 8:41, 42.

Jesus' encounter with the woman who was bleeding occurred while He was en route to Jairus' house.

3. (a) Who was Jairus (what position did he hold)?

(b) What was his immediate need?

4. What words in Matthew 9:18, Mark 5:22, 23, and Luke 8:41
   reveal Jairus' attitude as He approached Jesus?

Jairus' need was urgent, and he was well aware of his own
fear and helplessness. Approaching Jesus was unconventional
for this respected religious ruler, but desperate situations drive
individuals to implore help even from sources they had previ-
ously discounted. In that moment, Jairus could not have seen
himself as a leader who supervised worship services, exercised
care over the synagogue, and was responsible for the happenings of his congregation. Instead, his vocational role paled in
the shadow of his primary role as a father, the man personally
responsible for the care of an only child.

After Jairus made his desperate plea to Jesus and Jesus
agreed to go with him to his home, he must have had great
hope. Instead of arriving home in record time, however, they
were delayed when a woman touched Jesus. Imagine Jairus'
burning anxiety and annoyance. He wanted to dismiss Jesus'
question to the crowd about who had touched Him. Instead,
Jesus carried on a conversation with the woman and took time
to heal and restore her.

5. By the time Jesus finished talking to the woman He healed,
   who had arrived and with what message?

Even in Jairus' impatience to continue walking to his house, imagine the hope the woman's healing must have given him. Having just witnessed that healing, he wanted Jesus to arrive at his house before it was too late. But Jairus' hope turned to despair, as Jesus was still talking to the woman when the dreaded message arrived. This father's greatest fear had become a reality, and now his messenger discouraged him from taking any more of Jesus' time and attention.

6. What words did Jesus speak to Jairus (Mark 5:36)?

When Jairus first approached Jesus, he evidenced faith in Him, fell down at His feet, and begged Him to go to his house—and this was before he witnessed Jesus heal the woman who touched His clothing. Whether Jairus recognized Jesus as the Messiah or simply had confidence in His healing abilities because of what he had seen and heard, he was certain that Jesus could heal his daughter.

In commanding the action of belief (Mark 5:36), Jesus entreated Jairus to follow the woman's example. But with the devastating news about his daughter, it would have been easy for Jairus to lose whatever belief or faith had prompted him to approach Jesus. He had believed Jesus could heal his daughter. Now it was crucial for Jairus to maintain that belief. That he continued the walk to his house with Jesus shows that he held on to some hope.

Though the crowd continued to accompany Jesus, Jairus, and several disciples, at some point along the way Jesus dismissed them or forbid them from going all the way onto the property or into the house (Mark 5:37).

Arriving at the house, they found a noisy crowd. Matthew mentions musicians (Matthew 9:23). Mark states there was a tumult (Mark 5:38). Loud weeping and wailing usually followed a death as a show of respect. Because of Jairus' public position within the community, it is likely that many neighbors and acquaintances had already arrived and were in his home displaying anguish and grief.

   7. (a) Who did Jesus allow to witness His interaction with the twelve-year-old girl?

      (b) What did Jesus say to those who were already in the house?

Those gathered in the house knew that the girl had died. Her life was gone; she was physically dead. When Jesus countered what they comprehended to be true, it seemed absurd, and they responded with mockery and scoffing. Perhaps their unbelief was a factor in Jesus' preventing their presence while He interacted with the girl.

Instead of agreeing with the crowd, Jesus stated that the girl was sleeping. This was the reality, because Jesus knew that her present condition was temporary and that He would shortly overturn it. This is the first time the Bible records Jesus making a statement about a dead person sleeping, but it is not the last. A similar statement is recorded in John 11:11 when Jesus said, "Our friend Lazarus sleeps, but I go that I may wake him up." Because of Jesus' power and according to His will, raising this girl and Lazarus from the dead was no more difficult than waking someone from sleep.

   8. According to Matthew 9:25, Mark 5:41, and Luke 8:54, what did Jesus do and say as He approached Jairus' daughter?

Jesus took the dead girl's hand, an act that defied ceremonial law. Jesus had not become unclean when He touched the bier of the widow of Nain's son. Nor did He become unclean when the bleeding woman touched Him. And He did not become unclean when He touched this girl's hand. Though Jesus could have healed her without a physical touch, He showed personal compassion by taking her hand.

Both Mark and Luke quote the words Jesus spoke to the girl. Mark recorded them in the original Aramaic, while Luke's words were translated into Greek for the benefit of Gentile readers. The girl's spirit was revived and reentered her body at the moment Jesus spoke to her, and her illness left her. Just as with Peter's mother-in-law and the woman who was bleeding, the girl was completely restored without any residual weakness.

Though Jesus' direct interaction was with the twelve-year-old girl, her mother was also present and included by Jesus as one of the witnesses to His miracle. In the same way that Jesus brought the dead son of the widow of Nain back to life yet gave the greatest gift to his mother, He also gave a great gift to the unnamed mother of this girl. The gospel writers did not record this mother's response, yet Jesus gifted her with the life of her daughter as well as with the privilege of believing in Him.

As Jesus instructed the girl's astonished parents to give her something to eat, He also instructed them not to publicize what had happened (Mark 5:42, 43). What a difficult command to honor! Perhaps Jesus wanted to leave the area before news of this miracle reached those who opposed Him. Perhaps He wanted to minimize sensationalism and protect the girl and her parents from excessive attention. Perhaps He wanted the focus of His public ministry to be on His words rather than on healing miracles. At the same time, an entire crowd was gathered outside Jairus' house, and it would have been impossible to keep them from knowing about the resurrection of this girl's body.

9. What reason for Jesus' instruction not to tell others seems the most likely and viable?

Personal Reflection

Put yourself in Jairus' place. He had made his desperate request to Jesus. Jesus had agreed to go with him to his home, but He seemed to move too slowly while giving attention and help to others. Perhaps you have taken a personal need to Jesus in prayer but are tempted to despair because He has not yet worked a solution.

10. If you are a follower of Jesus Christ, one who wants to keep learning from Him, what lesson from this account do you want to implement?

11. What do you think Jesus wants you to learn?

12. Think about the girl's mother. She was an inaudible character in this account, yet she participated as a witness to the miracle. Has God assigned you to quietly watch Him work in someone you love dearly? In what ways can you hear and heed the words of Jesus to Jairus, "Do not be afraid; only believe"?

13. Reflect upon your own salvation. Remember the day Jesus breathed new life into your dead spirit. That miracle was as powerful as His revivification (making alive again) of this girl. Write a prayer of thanksgiving for God's work of giving you new life. Ask Him to give you revival in specific areas of need.

The Canaanite Woman and the Woman Caught in Adultery
Women Who Were Outsiders

PART 1
The Canaanite Woman from Syrophoenicia

I AM REMINDED of a time when one of my children had such a significant need that I was desperate to find help. As a teenager, my daughter was in a small African country when her belongings, including her passport, were stolen from her host missionary's car. There was no Internet access, and the place she served was thirty miles from a telephone. Since she was scheduled to return to the United States about two weeks later, I became desperate to find help from a distance. I contacted officials whom I didn't know; I asked questions I had never before considered; I begged for help. I was turned away, given flimsy excuses, and shown little sympathy; yet I still begged.

Personal Recall

1. Recall a time when your heartache and fatigue made you desperate. Perhaps it happened because of concern for a child or your own personal need.

Personal Discovery

When Jesus went to Tyre and Sidon to gain rest for His disciples, their time was interrupted by the cries of a desperate woman from Syrophoenicia. Both Matthew and Mark record the incident.

Read Mark 7:24–30.

2. Where was Jesus when this woman located Him?

3. What was the woman's request and her follow-up plea?

Read Matthew 15:22–28.

4. (a) According to Matthew 15:22–28, how did Jesus initially respond?

(b) She worshiped Jesus and asked for help again (v. 25). Then what did He say (v. 26)?

Jesus told the Syrophoenician woman that it was not right to take bread from children in order to give it to dogs. He meant that she had no right to take blessings intended for Jewish people; she needed to understand this before Jesus could help her. In spite of racial, social, cultural, and spiritual barriers, the woman showed understanding and discernment: she knew Jesus' mission and was asking for what others had rejected.

5. How did the woman respond to Jesus' reply (Matthew 15:27)?

This woman showed significant perseverance. In spite of Jesus' initial answer, she was not discouraged. She agreed with Jesus and asked for only a crumb. In doing so, she acknowledged that as a Gentile she was not the target of Jesus' mission and was not entitled to have what she asked for, yet she persisted in asking for her child's healing.

6. On what basis was her child healed (Matthew 15:28)?

Jesus responded to the mother's humility and persistence. In this case, He did not see, touch, or speak to the girl, but healed her immediately as her mother demonstrated faith that He was the Messiah.

Personal Reflection

7. What did you learn about prayer from this woman's words and her plea?

PART 2
The Woman Caught in Adultery

I recall a time when I was "caught in the act" of a lie. To make it worse, I was convinced that I must defend my lie at all costs to protect myself and others. We were involved in a scheme we thought would not be exposed. I told more lies in multiple attempts to cover myself, but the truth was made known. I experienced shame instead of the triumph I had anticipated. Adding to my shame and regret were my companions, who deserted me and tattled on me, exposing my sin and leaving me to bear the consequences alone.

Personal Recall

8. Recall a time when you were caught in the act of a sin
   and experienced the embarrassment and shame of your
   wrongdoing.

We don't usually think about shame being a way to draw
near to God. Instead, it makes us want to hide and focus on
our defeat. In the throes of shame, it is difficult to see a way to
approach the Lord, yet He is our hope of forgiveness and grace.

Personal Discovery

Read John 8:1–11.

John 8:1–11 introduces another unnamed woman. No details are given about her family or her history. We see her, however, in one of the more difficult scenarios we can imagine.

9. In addition to shame, what are some of the emotions you
   think this woman might have experienced when she met
   Jesus?

Just before Jesus met her, He spent time alone on the Mount
of Olives, where He talked with His Father. From there He went
to the temple to teach.

Many people seemed to expect Jesus to go to the temple, so
they went there to hear Him (John 8:2). While He was teaching, scribes and Pharisees (religious leaders), who also seemed
to know where He would be, brought a woman to Him in the
middle of the courtyard. They accused her of adultery and said
they had caught her in the act. They reminded Jesus that the
law of Moses said she should be stoned (vv. 3, 4).

Among other lies, our culture has accepted the lie that

adultery is a personal choice that can be pursued for one's own satisfaction or for someone else's gain. The Bible portrays it as a snare, a temptation that will result in great personal loss, and it instructs us to run away from it. Though adultery is never good or right, many women and girls in our world are trapped by it. They have been caught in a snare that has used them as bait.

If you are able to access the *Gospel of John* film, please watch the video clip of this account. This film is available on DVD in many libraries, and the account can be viewed on YouTube at www.youtube.com/watch?v=0ylFgewaFcM.

Several significant pieces of this story are not provided in Scripture, so some questions beg to be asked. We will ask and answer four of them.

How was this woman caught in the act?

First, we wonder, how was this woman caught in the act? It seems likely that the whole scenario was a setup. That the religious leaders grabbed this woman and headed straight for Jesus, knowing exactly where He would be at that moment, hints at premeditation and conspiracy.

10. According to Leviticus 20:10, what law did the woman break, and what was the penalty for breaking that law?

11. According to John 8:4–6, what was the reason for the religious leaders' scheme?

What kind of trap were they setting for Jesus, and what were the accusations they hoped to make?

We have to wonder why the religious leaders thought this particular trap would work. The woman was being used as bait. By asking Jesus to choose between the law of Moses and His reputation for compassion and forgiveness, they thought they had a scheme for which there would be no escape. If Jesus rejected the law of Moses, His credibility as a religious teacher would be compromised. If He upheld the Mosaic law, His reputation for compassion and forgiveness would be questioned. These religious leaders dared Jesus to answer correctly.

Before Him that morning stood a woman unquestionably guilty of a serious offense. There was no way Jesus could question the validity of the accusation, and there is no evidence that He did. The woman had been caught in the act; there were witnesses; the woman herself was not denying the charge: her guilt was indisputable.

Either way Jesus answered, the religious leaders would have reason to accuse Him. If He answered, "Stone her," He would have convicted this woman to death. In the culture of that day, only the Roman government had that authority, so Jesus would have been countering the Roman government. If He had answered, "Let her go," He would have been teaching disobedience to the law of Moses. As a Jewish man and the Messiah, Jesus had a solemn obligation to respect this law.

Jesus answered them in a way that is often needed—with silence.

Where was the man?

Since adultery cannot be committed alone, there is reason to wonder about the man involved in this woman's sin.

12. What does Leviticus 20:10 say about the consequences for the man?

Unless the man managed to overpower and get away from the religious leaders, a double standard was being used. It is feasible that the man was even a willing party to the scheme.

Jesus stopped the accusers by writing something in the dirt (John 8:6, 8), which brings up the next question.

What did Jesus write?

This is the only time the Bible records Jesus writing something, but it does not disclose what He wrote. It is unknown whether He wrote the same thing both times or two separate messages. Perhaps He wrote a partial list of some of the leaders' sins. Perhaps He wrote the Ten Commandments. Perhaps He wrote their names in fulfillment of Jeremiah 17:13: "Those who depart from Me shall be written in the earth." John is clear that Jesus wrote with His finger in the dust of the ground, but no one knows the words.

13. What did Jesus say in addition to writing on the ground?

Clearly, the Jewish leaders who had conspired to entrap the Lord had not anticipated this response. It caught them unawares, and suddenly they were "on trial" before the crowd. According to Jewish law, in any case involving capital punishment, the witnesses must begin the stoning.

14. What did Jesus ask the woman?

15. How did the woman answer?

16. What words of instruction did Jesus speak to her?

The order of Christ's words is important. Note that He did not say, "Sin no more, and then I won't condemn you." By forgiving her first, He gifted her with hope. Think about the three gifts Jesus gave this woman through response to her situation:

- Hope—This gift might be called "grace," "compassion," "mercy," or "love." Jesus did not condemn the woman, but neither did He condone her sin. She was guilty before God. She knew it, and He knew it. He did not cover up her sin, but He gave her hope by calling her to repentance.

- Instruction—Then Jesus gave her the responsibility to refrain from sin from that point forward. Even so, He didn't assign a disciple to keep an eye on her, and He didn't put her on probation. He told her the truth, and by doing so, He challenged her heart.

Hope + Instruction = a combination
for effecting transformation

- Opportunity for healing through repentance—This is, perhaps, the greatest of the three gifts. The woman was someone Christ came to seek and to save. Today He does not condone sin, but He offers cleansing rather than condemnation.

This accounts shows the power of the gospel message. We are truly guilty in the eyes of the holy God. Because of sin, we are caught by God's justice and deserve death. As sinners, we are helpless and unable to change our condition. We are condemned by conscience, true moral guilt, and often by others. But then Jesus steps in to rescue us.

Are we listening? Do we "hear" Jesus Christ offer His gifts of hope, instruction, and opportunity for repentance and healing because He has already died for us? Do we recognize the sin in our lives and hear Him tell us to stop sinning? Do we hear Him tell us that He no longer condemns us? Do we hear His compassion toward us? Do we hear Him offer the freedom of forgiveness if we confess our sin? Do we hear Him as He extends mercy, grace, reconciliation, and cleansing?

17. (a) Write out Romans 8:1, 31–34.

(b) What is your response to the truths in these verses?

What a gift it was to this woman that she was taken to Jesus rather than to the officials. Jesus responded in a countercultural way by not treating her as a man's property, but as a person of value. He showed respect by speaking to her with tenderness, compassion, and forgiveness. Jesus acted within the full degree of the law, but His answer to the teachers of the law caused them to back down from condemning her. Jesus taught that no sin is too great for God to forgive and that a pattern of sinful behavior can be changed.

Personal Reflection

18. The record of Jesus' interaction with this woman is quite sobering, yet it speaks loudly to many of us. Even though John did not tell any details about her family, history, or the situation surrounding her sin, it is clear that she met Jesus Christ personally and experienced His forgiveness and kindness. At a fearful moment in her life, this woman saw Jesus' wisdom in action and heard Him speak. When you were caught in the act of a sin and experienced the embarrassment and shame of your wrongdoing, what truth was most meaningful to you?

19. Which of the gifts that Jesus communicated to the woman
do you need most? Why?

20. How can you change your approach toward someone who
needs hope, instruction, and/or an opportunity to heal
through repentance?

Mary and Martha
Women Who
Worshiped and Served

IT'S A STRUGGLE TO BALANCE LIFE . . . family . . . meals . . .
ministries . . . Bible study . . . laundry . . . personal worship . . .
groceries . . . prayer . . . housecleaning . . . hospitality . . . employ-
ment . . . friendships . . . paying bills. My list just keeps going,
and I reevaluate my priorities on a regular basis. The tension
between serving and worshiping is a daily reality. I want to
worship more. I want to sit and pray. I want to read my Bible
and study without interruptions. But I also cannot neglect my
responsibilities.

If you are like me, how can we worship while serving? How
can we have what Jesus called in Luke 10:42 the "good part"?

Personal Recall

1. What do you know about Mary and Martha? What character traits are well known about each of them?

2. When you think of Mary and Martha, do you think of yourself as being more like one of them than the other? If so,
   which one?

Personal Discovery

Mary and Martha were sisters living with their brother, Lazarus, in Bethany. Martha probably was the eldest. Their home was located only two miles from Jerusalem.

Read Luke 10:38–42.

   3. What do you observe in Luke 10:38–42?

Martha

Martha was the hostess on this occasion. Perhaps she fussed with unnecessary details, but she felt the weight of responsibility. She also had quite a house full of people. Though the text is not specific about how many people arrived, it does say that Jesus had His disciples with Him. That would be a minimum of thirteen, but it is likely there were more, since Jesus frequently traveled with female disciples and other followers as well.

Consider how you would respond if thirteen or more people showed up for a meal and lodging. If you have traveled to other countries and been a houseguest, you may have experienced being hosted by people who have less materially than you have. It is a humbling privilege to be received with honor in such places. As I have had that privilege, I have learned much about the unimportance of the things I fuss about and the things that keep me from giving hospitality with joy and generosity.

While in Moldova in 2008, our teaching team, made up of three couples and another man, arrived at a church building on a Sunday afternoon to teach pastors and their wives for the next week. After the evening service, the small congregation was asked for volunteers to host us for a full week, giving us lodging and breakfast and dinner each day. I was convicted as I wondered if I would have volunteered—without going to the grocery store or vacuuming. The family with whom my husband and I stayed had very little, but they shared it with joy.

That day in Bethany, Mary was present, but this passage records only Jesus' personal interaction with Martha.

4. Consider a possible scenario in your own home. How might you respond if one of your children approached you and said, "Mom, she's not helping me clean up because she's having her devotions"?

5. From Luke 10:38–42, what do you learn or observe about Mary?

6. For what did Jesus correct Martha?

7. What did Martha learn?

While Martha worked on preparations, most likely for a meal, Mary sat at Jesus' feet listening to Him teach. This prompted frustration in Martha. Perhaps she was bothered more about not being able to sit and listen too—after all, she had chores to do—than she was in having to work alone. Sometimes in wanting to free ourselves for a preferred activity, we need to be careful to guard against jealousy and trying to rob others of their enjoyment.

Jesus did not correct Martha for doing her work, but for being too concerned about outward things. She was worried and troubled as she allowed her responsibilities to rob her of her joy and gracious spirit. Jesus appreciated her hospitality, but He made it clear to her that Mary had chosen the correct priority.

In this scenario, Martha was so busy doing good tasks that she neglected to spend enough time with the Lord. Christian women are especially challenged with the temptation and danger of being too busy to continue growing in their relationship with Jesus. It is crucial to find the appropriate balance between serving and spending time in study.

In the January 18 devotional in *My Utmost for His Highest*, Oswald Chambers says, "The greatest competitor of true devotion to Jesus is the service we do for Him. It is easier to serve than to pour out our lives completely for Him."

Mary

8. What words did Jesus use to commend Mary (v. 42)?

Though any words Jesus may have spoken directly to Mary are not recorded here, He applauded her choice to learn from Him as a disciple. It is obvious from her choice and actions that she was eager to learn from Him and that she understood true devotion.

The "good part" (Luke 10:42) that Mary chose can be summarized as "the truths learned from time with Jesus that cannot be taken from us." The things the Lord teaches us during our times of reading and listening to His Word are precious and well worth our focused attention.

This account of Martha serving Jesus in her home is the first of three passages in which Jesus interacted with the two sisters. This particular story is suspended before the readers know how Martha responded to Jesus or how Mary and Martha reconciled the tension between them. Within several months of this interaction between Jesus and Martha, their brother died. Jesus arrived back in Bethany days later.

Read John 11:1–44.

Though each of the sisters saw Jesus at different times, each of them said the same thing to Him as they greeted Him upon His return: "If You had been here, my brother would not have died." Both of them believed that Jesus could and would have healed Lazarus if He had arrived sooner.

Martha

Read John 11:20–28.

When Martha heard that Jesus was coming, she left her work and went to Him immediately, reaching Him while He was still outside her village. She had a personal conversation with Him before she called Mary.

9. What do you observe about the interaction between Jesus and Martha?

Martha showed genuine confidence in Jesus as the One Who could work miracles and Who had a close connection to God. She also expressed belief in the coming resurrection, but was that enough?

Jesus was not content to leave Martha with only a partial comprehension of the final resurrection, so He led her into fuller understanding of the truth. After assuring her that her brother would live again (John 11:23), He led her to an understanding that He was the Christ, the Son of God, the One Who was to come into the world (v. 25).

Do you see that Martha had a statement of faith, but she also needed a lesson in faith? Her heart was right in that she believed in Jesus and trusted in His power to heal, but, though she recognized His power, she didn't understand His deity until He corrected her.

Many women believe that Jesus exists; they even pray. But they are not true believers in the fact that Jesus is God, that

He alone is our hope and Savior, and that He is the only way to God and to eternal life in Heaven. Others of us truly have a personal relationship with Jesus Christ, but we still struggle to demonstrate that belief when the Lord allows into our lives something that stretches us with what I call a "lesson of faith."

When we read God's Word, there is powerful and personal benefit in asking, Do I believe this? At the time that question confronts our hearts, a decision must be made. The actions that follow correspond with the choice we made. When Jesus asked Martha that penetrating question, she chose to believe, and she understood that Jesus really is God, the resurrection and the life.

Mary

Read again John 11:28–36. When Mary saw and reached Jesus, her grief was obvious (v. 32). As she spoke the same words to Him that Martha had, He was moved with compassion and sympathy (v. 33). He was also troubled by her lack of understanding about Him. Observe how gently Jesus moved her (as well as Martha) into a deeper relationship with Himself.

10. What reason did the Jewish comforters give for Jesus' weeping (John 11:36)?

11. What do you think prompted Jesus to weep?

12. What did Jesus do next (John 11:38–45)?

Consider the fact that this account is recorded in scripture with much detail. Perhaps it is preserved as an example showing that God sometimes allows the innocent to suffer as a means of demonstrating His glory. There is no reason to think that Mary and Martha suffered such a great loss due to any wrongdoing;

it was a loss that is part of life. Through it we can see God being glorified and individuals being stretched in their faith.

When Jesus saw Mary and other Jews weeping, He groaned within Himself and He wept. Consider the awful emotional grief of those observers who did not see Jesus as Life. It seems likely that Jesus wept out of grief because they did not understand. There was such conflict with sin and death. He was angry with the tyranny of Satan that brought sorrow and death through sin, and Jesus wept over its tragic consequences.

What a powerful lesson for us! God allows those who love Him to suffer as a means of showing His glory to those who do not yet believe.

The Gospels record one more visit in which Jesus interacted with Mary and Martha. The night before Jesus rode into Jerusalem on a donkey and proclaimed Himself king of Israel, He was a dinner guest at the home of Simon the leper. Though both sisters were present during this third encounter, only the words Jesus spoke to Mary are recorded.

Read Matthew 26:6–13; Mark 14:3–9; John 12:1–8.

At this dinner, Mary poured an entire jar of expensive perfume on Jesus' head (Matthew 26:7). This provoked some indignation and objection (vv. 8, 9). It also highlighted the contrast between Mary's insight and devotion and the disciples' pragmatism and lack of understanding.

13. Why were some of the disciples critical of Mary's action (Mark 14:4, 5)?

14. How did Jesus respond to the disciples' objections (Mark 14:6–9)?

15. What understanding about Jesus' future did Mary's action demonstrate (John 12:7)?

Jesus accepted Mary's extravagant worship. He commended Mary for serving Him according to her capacity and ability and for doing it out of insight and devotion. Finally, He defended her in a way that went against their culture by declaring to the men that her action was good.

Though this account focuses on Mary's action, John 12 mentions Martha's presence. Do you notice what she was doing? She was serving . . . still serving, but in a place of peace and calm, without any complaint. As she served, she facilitated Mary's opportunity for worship. Martha's service was her way of expressing love; she delighted in meeting needs.

Learning what Jesus wants to teach us and growing through it is our goal. It is not necessary for us to choose between being a Mary or a Martha. What we learn from both of them is that we need to worship before we are equipped to serve. In the same way, we need to serve after we have worshiped.

Personal Reflection

16. What is your plan for choosing the "good part"? How do you spend time listening to Jesus every day?

17. What truth have you experienced during the past week that you would not have learned apart from spending time reading God's Word?

18. How could you simplify or streamline your life to allow yourself to choose the good part?

19. How do you demonstrate your love for and worship of the Lord in an extravagant and unreserved way?

A Woman in a Crowd and Salome
Women Who Should Have Remained Quiet

I RECALL A FEW TIMES when I spoke up, believing I was making a true statement of praise to someone, only to realize that I was unaware of the depth of the situation. When I was able to see more of the complete picture, my impulsive compliment seemed trite, and it didn't really express the level of acknowledgment that was appropriate.

PART 1
A Woman in a Crowd

Personal Recall

1. When have you spoken up to praise or encourage someone only to find out that you were offering a shallow compliment instead of a more thoughtful acclaim?

2. When, if ever, have you been corrected for praising the wrong person?

Personal Discovery

Luke 11:14 records that Jesus delivered a man from a mute demon, which allowed the man to speak. Instead of praising Jesus, some of the observers attributed that exorcism to Satan's power (v. 15). Others tested Jesus by asking for an additional sign from Heaven (v. 16). In response, Jesus made strong statements about the fake exorcists who practiced phony exorcisms. Instead of giving true deliverance to an individual, the messengers of Satan only grant a respite to the demons, who will possess others as well (vv. 24–26).

Read Luke 11:27 and 28.

3. Luke 11:27 says, "As He spoke these things. . . ." Of what things was Jesus speaking?

Nothing is known about the woman in the crowd who shouted out a compliment. Her words were those of praise, but they fell short of what would please Jesus. Though she seemed to recognize His power and greatness, her praise was directed toward His mother.

4. What did the woman say?

5. Jesus gently corrected the woman. What did He say (Luke 11:28)?

The woman's compliment was a sincere one of admiration. She spoke truth, yet her focus was shallow, and she missed the significance of Jesus' full identity. She admired His wisdom and power, yet her praise targeted something lesser than the reality of His deity.

It is significant that Jesus did not ignore the woman's comment or allow it to stand unchallenged. While it is true that there is blessing in having a connection with Jesus—whether as physical family or as those who have been adopted by Him—there is far greater blessing in hearing His Word, meditating on it, and being changed by it. Yes, Mary was blessed by the privilege of being His mother, but her greatest blessing was anchored in being one of His disciples.

Personal Reflection

I have been guilty many times of seeing Jesus through the grid of my own need, my own desires, and my own narrow view of significance. I need to be careful not to focus on just part of Who He is—perhaps an outstanding teacher, a good man, or a respectable example. Rather, I should focus on Him as my Savior, my Lord, and the One I worship and obey.

6. In what ways might your perspective of Jesus be limited?

7. Think of specific people you want to encourage. How can you give them appropriate recognition and praise without shortchanging Jesus from the praise He deserves in the situation?

PART 2
Salome, a Mother with a Request

Personal Recall

8. Recall a time when you watched or overheard a woman asking an unreasonable request of her child.

9. When have you asked God for something without realizing all of the ramifications? What difficult thing happened because He answered yes?

Salome *[handwritten annotation in left margin]*

Personal Discovery

Matthew 4:21, 22 and Mark 1:19, 20 record Jesus' call to James and John. Both passages cite Zebedee as their father. Mark 15:40 names their mother, while Matthew, recording the same scenario, refers to her only as the mother of Zebedee's sons (Matthew 27:56). When these passages are laid side-by-side, it becomes clear that the mother of James and John, Zebedee's sons, is called Salome.

Read Mark 15:40 and 41.

10. How is Salome identified?

One who followed Jesus + ministered to Him. *[handwritten]*

Read Matthew 20:17–21.

11. What request did Salome present to Jesus?

12. What did her body language and the words of her request indicate about her belief in Jesus?

Look carefully at verses 17–19. Salome made her request during a journey to Jerusalem with Jesus and all twelve of the disciples. She also made her request after Jesus predicted His death and resurrection.

Compare Matthew 19:28–30. There is no doubt that the disciples remembered Jesus' words when He spoke of thrones in His kingdom. They recognized Jesus as One Who would be a king, governing a kingdom. Yet their lack of understanding was obvious, as ruling in His kingdom became a priority in their thoughts.

When Salome appealed to Jesus, she was asking with the ambition of an earthly or temporal time frame. As a mother, she was most attentive to the aspirations she had for her own sons to be honored by Jesus. She was unable to understand that her request would not coincide with the glory of God and that it held consequences she and her sons would be unable to meet.

Read Matthew 20:22, 23.

13. How did Jesus respond to Salome's request (Matthew 20:22, 23)? He said no.

James and John were present and seemed to agree with their mother's request, believing they would be able to do whatever Jesus asked of them. In His response, Jesus took Salome's question as an opportunity to explain truth to her sons and the other disciples about the goal of being servants.

Read Matthew 20:23, 25–28.

In an attempt to help them recognize their foolish and inappropriate ambition, Jesus spoke to them about the cross, about the suffering He would0 yet endure (Matthew 20:23). It's interesting that He did not rebuke Salome but redirected her thinking to the priority of serving rather than ruling and being served (vv. 25–28).

14. When James and John said they would be able to go through whatever Jesus would go through, He told them that they would indeed (Matthew 20:23). Who did He say would determine who would sit on either side of His throne?

who, His Father chose.

Read Mark 15:40, 41 and Mark 16:1.

15. What can you discern about Salome's continued devotion
    to Jesus?

Personal Reflection

Salome evidenced her true devotion to Jesus Christ. She
was one of the women who followed Him from Galilee, supporting Him and caring for His needs. She was at the cross,
staying to see where He was buried, and she arrived at the
tomb the morning He arose from the dead.

Consider the question Jesus asked in His response to Salome: "Are you able to drink the cup that I am about to drink,
and be baptized with the baptism that I am baptized with?"
That question prompts our personal evaluation of our commitment and perseverance regarding suffering, obedience, and
service.

16. Write a prayer of commitment to the Lord that expresses
    your honest yet hopeful commitment to Him as you pledge
    yourself to follow His plan for you no matter what it holds.

The Woman with a Spirit of Infirmity and the Daughters of Jerusalem
Women Who Got a Second Chance

MY PRAYER LIST IS LONG. I am asking God to do a plethora of things. I have the privilege of interceding for many people. A number of my requests have been ongoing for years, decades even. What a blessing and great reward I receive when my specific prayers are answered in the ways I had dreamed. On the other hand, God shows great kindness and amazing work when He answers a need for which I haven't even asked. As I reflect upon many of the things God has done for me, I realize I didn't even pray about many of them. I didn't know what I needed or what He could do. I didn't expect the blessings He gave me.

PART 1
The Woman with a Spirit of Infirmity

Personal Recall

1. What is a recent blessing God gave you for which you did not ask?

Perhaps you are acquainted with a woman who has been trapped for years by physical limitations. Can you empathize with her as you stop to think of the boundaries that hem her in because of a disease or disability? Think of the things you are able to do on a daily basis that are not possible for her. Over the years, it has been interesting for me to note that some of these women are often more content than those who do not have the same challenges.

Personal Discovery

Read Luke 13:10–17.

Only Luke—a physician concerned with physical conditions who was especially attentive to Jesus' miracles of merciful healing—wrote down and preserved the event. He was careful to communicate an accurate diagnosis of this unnamed woman's long-term plight.

2. What words or details communicate that this woman's condition was more than a physical problem?

It is most likely that this woman's physical body was crippled to the point of being grotesque. Luke 13:11 says she was bent over and unable to rise up, so it seems she was unable even to lift her head enough to look at Jesus' face. Though her physical body showed abnormality and even deformity, the text makes it clear that the cause of her problem was some kind of evil spirit. Because Jesus did not rebuke her or a demon, it is not likely she was demon possessed, but Jesus made it clear that her painful disorder was because of Satan's evil work. Luke specifically calls her condition "a spirit of infirmity," and Jesus told the synagogue ruler that the woman had been bound by Satan for the entire term of her malady.

3. Where was Jesus when He encountered this woman?

4. What did Jesus do or say to this infirm woman?

5. Is there evidence that the woman had any faith in Jesus
   Christ?

No one advocated for this woman. In contrast to the healings of many people who had been brought to Jesus and for
whom His help had been sought, Jesus Himself singled out this
woman.

It's interesting that when Jesus healed her, He used the
word "loosed" instead of "healed" or "made well." When He
spoke and laid His hands on her, He indicated He was releas-
ing her from bondage (Luke 13:12, 13, 16). Jesus did not speak
to a demon or show any sign of exorcism in this case, yet He
made it clear that He was freeing this woman who didn't even
ask for anything. He gave her a second chance at health and
personal freedom.

6. How did the woman respond to the freedom Jesus gave her
   (Luke 13:13)?

7. Why was there opposition to Jesus' act of kindness (Luke
   13:14)?

As part of the Ten Commandments, God instructed His
people to remember the Sabbath and to keep it holy. Over time,
this commandment was modified in a way that added extra
rules. Since medical care usually was enlisted from physicians,

the Jewish religious leaders added a prohibition about healing, because they said it constituted work. Clearly, they did not understand that the work of Jesus Christ was above any prohibition they added.

This was not the first time one of Jesus' miracles provoked a controversy over Sabbath traditions. This account in Luke 13 is the sixth of seven times Jesus performed a healing miracle on the Sabbath, though the accounts of His exorcising a demon and healing Peter's mother-in-law, a lame man at the Bethesda Pool, and the man with dropsy did not take place in a synagogue.

A comparable miracle inside a synagogue had, however, taken place much earlier in Jesus' public ministry. While He was in Galilee, He restored a man's withered hand on the Sabbath (Matthew 12:9–14). The Pharisees were indignant in this case of healing as well and accused Him of doing what was unlawful. When Jesus responded in favor of the value of human life, His accusers determined to destroy Him.

In Luke 13 Jesus approached this crippled woman in another synagogue and in the presence of the synagogue ruler. His response was similar to the one recorded in Matthew. Jesus publicly showed concern and regard for someone others had shunned. In doing so, Jesus personally contrasted His new way of life with the old legalistic, pharisaical restrictions.

  8. Whom did the ruler address in response to Jesus' action, and what did he say?

  9. If concern for the people had been this Jewish leader's priority, how might we expect him to have responded? Write a brief script of an acceptable reaction.

10. How did Jesus respond to the ruler (Luke 13:15, 16)?

On a day set aside to give focused attention to God, Jesus met added opposition to His work of mercy and compassion. The ruler and his cohorts were arrogant and accusing, and Jesus revealed their legalism and hypocrisy. This was the last time Luke recorded Jesus teaching in a synagogue.

Consider the following questions raised by the ruler's words, and determine whether what he said had any validity. The ruler implied that six days were available for healing. This makes me wonder how many healings actually happened in that synagogue. Also, could people be healed if Jesus were not present? Was the ruler suggesting that the woman's healing was available another time? Could she have returned for healing the next day? If so, why had she not come on one of those days during the past eighteen years? Or, if she had, why hadn't she been healed?

11. (a) What phrase did Jesus use to identify the woman to the ruler?

(b) What significance is there to this description?

When Jesus declared that the ruler was a hypocrite, He was making a powerful statement. Rather than promoting worship and teaching, the man was trying to squelch it and shut it down. It seems he routinely sanctioned breaking the Sabbath for the benefit of an animal, but not for the health and restoration of this woman.

The Jewish leader's care was ironic, selective, and self-centered. The man sanctioned loosing a donkey so it could drink, but wanted to prohibit Jesus from loosing a woman's bondage. In contrast, Jesus taught that helping a person is more important than helping an animal. In doing so, He acknowledged the woman as a daughter of Abraham, one of God's Chosen People and an heir of the promises given to Abraham.

Personal Reflection

12. Name a woman within your sphere of influence who is often ignored and unheard, but has a need that could be changed by the freedom offered in Jesus Christ. Summarize her situation.

13. How can you show kindness to her and communicate that she has value in God's eyes and yours?

PART 2
The Daughters of Jerusalem

On the way to His crucifixion at Calvary, Jesus turned to a small segment of the crowd that followed Him as they mourned and lamented Him. His address of them is interesting, as He offered a caution.

Read Luke 23:26–31.

14. What caution did Jesus give these women?

Public mourning was common during the time Jesus lived on earth. Rather than being true disciples, it is likely that these women were not those who had traveled with Him and cared for His needs as He journeyed from Galilee. This would mean they were not the same ones mentioned later in Luke 23:49 as those who watched His crucifixion and observed His burial.

Instead, it is more likely these women were part of a common crowd of observers as Jesus passed by their segment of the city. It is also probable they had heard Him teach and they wanted to express their sympathy at the time of His imminent execution.

Jesus' reply to them was a prophetic warning that seems to point toward the tragedy and destruction of Jerusalem that would occur in AD 70. Those who were young mothers when Jesus addressed them would have ranged between fifty and seventy years of age at the time of the massacre by the Romans in AD 66 and the persecution that followed.

Israel had rejected Jesus as their Messiah, so He was on the way to the cross, His kingdom postponed. Because of these things, the Jews would face future tribulation. Jesus' warning presented the women with the opportunity for a second chance: they had rejected Him as their king, but if they believed what He was telling them, repented, and believed on Him as Messiah and Savior, they would belong in His future Kingdom.

Personal Reflection

Sometimes, I become very concerned about my grandchildren as I speculate on the trials they will face. The economic, political, medical, and moral temperature of our society certainly can be frightening, but God has given a mandate for families to continue. As we reflect upon the warning Jesus gave the "Daughters of Jerusalem," we realize that the world's condition has made every time period a precarious time.

15. Have you been ignoring a caution from God's Word? Do you need to receive Jesus as your Savior? Or, if you know Him, do you need to repent of a sinful action or attitude?

16. What three promises in God's Word do you want to re-member when you are tempted to fear for the generation succeeding you?

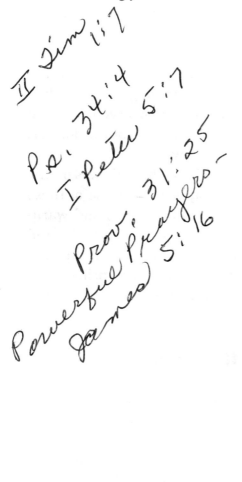

II Tim 1:7

Ps. 34:4

I Peter 5:7

Prov. 31:25

Powerful Prayers —
James 5:16

Mary Magdalene
A Woman Set Free

DISQUALIFIED—it has such a permanent, ugly, and hopeless ring to it. What disqualifies us from service to others and worship of Jesus? Several events from my own past have left me wondering if God would allow me another chance or if I might be put on a shelf and allowed nothing more than to observe the blessings of others. Do we really expect God to turn mourning into dancing and sorrow into joy (Job 41:22; John 16:20)?

One of the women who followed Jesus was Mary of Magdala, or Mary Magdalene, whom He had rescued from extreme bondage. She had not necessarily been an immoral woman, but she had been bound to a power greater than her own. The Bible does not mention her until after her first encounter with Jesus Christ.

Personal Recall

1. Recall a time when you experienced some kind of bondage. Do you remember the hopelessness and anxiety? Try to describe the freedom you knew after you were released from that physical, mental, or emotional enslavement.

Personal Discovery

Before Mary Met Jesus

Read Luke 8:1 and 2.

2. What do Mark 16:9 and Luke 8:1, 2 reveal about Mary Magdalene's life before she met Jesus?

Mary of Magdala had been possessed by demons. Before she met Jesus, she was under satanic influence and completely controlled by a demon or demons. Demon-possession is not possible for Christians, for we have the indwelling Holy Spirit (Romans 5:5; 1 Corinthians 6:19). John wrote, "He who is in you [the Spirit of God] is greater than he [Satan] who is in the world" (1 John 4:4).

In contrast to demon possession, demon oppression is unusual pressure from the outside that affects a person's health or ability to think or function clearly. This may be seen in abnormal fears, anxieties, or some form of depression.

3. Since Mary Magdalene had been demon possessed, what are some of the things she may have felt and experienced?

The Bible does not teach believers today to cast out demons, but it does tell us to be alert for satanic attacks (e.g., 1 Peter 5:8), and it gives instructions on how to resist them (e.g., Jams 4:7–10).

4. What specific instructions are found in the following passages?

(a) Ephesians 6:10–20

(b) 1 Peter 5:8, 9

After Mary Met Jesus

Jesus delivered Mary Magdalene from hopeless bondage. So from the time of her release, she followed Him. Instead of being identified as a demon-possessed woman, she became known as a woman "out of whom had come seven demons." She was a testimony of the power and work of God, and she became a beautiful example of one who followed the Shepherd closely.

Mary could have sunk into total despair because of her past life or present circumstances, but she rose above her past to serve God. She continued to be one of Jesus' faithful students and disciples. As a single woman of means, she lived in His shadow, traveling with Him, supporting Him, enjoying fellowship, and serving. She cooperated with Jesus as He replaced her crippling past with a transformed present and future. She followed Him from Galilee to the Cross and is mentioned fourteen times in the Gospels.

5. What do Matthew 27:54–56, Mark 15:39–41, and John 19:25 reveal about Mary Magdalene?

6. What do Matthew 27:61; 28:1 and Mark 15:45–47; 16:1 reveal about Mary's presence, attention, and care?

Read Matthew 28:1–7; Mark 16:9; Luke 24:1–11; John 20:1, 2, 10–18.

7. (a) According to Matthew 28:1–7, who spoke directly to Mary?

(b) What instructions did she receive?

When Mary, along with other women, went to the tomb on the third morning, she found the stone removed. After she followed the angel's instructions, she returned to the tomb, wept, and saw two angels seated where Jesus' body had been.

8. (a) What misunderstanding did Mary Magdalene have
   about Jesus?

(b) At what point did she recognize Him?

Jesus addressed Mary in two ways: First, He called her "woman" (John 20:15). With this salutation, He allowed her to represent all of humanity. Jesus continues to give a message to women today. Second, He called her Mary (v. 16). In speaking her name, Jesus allowed her to represent the individuality of the gospel and the way He deals with all who come to Him.

John 10:27 records Jesus as saying, "My sheep hear My voice, and I know them, and they follow Me." The sheep are those who belong to the Lord through the relationship of salvation. Earlier in the chapter, verse 3 says, "The sheep hear his voice; and he calls his own sheep by name and leads them out."

Jesus knows your name! This gives significance to a relationship with you. It supposes that you will listen when you hear Him call, that you will be attentive to His words as He speaks through the Bible, that you will understand what He says, and that you will obey.

9. Not only did Jesus say Mary's name, He gave her something
   to do. What assignment and authority did Jesus give to
   Mary?

Try to imagine being the first person the resurrected Lord Jesus appeared and spoke to. Though Mary Magdalene was the first then, Jesus speaks to believers today through His Word and by the indwelling Holy Spirit.

The resurrection of Jesus Christ was the most remarkable and significant event in the history of humanity. That Jesus went against Jewish culture and gave Mary Magdalene the license and authority to be the first to testify of His resurrection was exceptionally remarkable, since a woman's testimony was not even considered valid in a court of law.

Personal Reflection

10. Think of a few people you know who have been rescued by Jesus Christ from a life of significant addiction and bondage. What temptations have they faced that threatened to prevent them from moving forward?

11. Have you recognized Jesus as the One Who died to pay the penalty for your sin, and have you received Him as your Savior?

12. Write a prayer of thanksgiving for the fact that Jesus knows the name of each person who belongs to Him. In this prayer, you may want to refer to your own personal relationship with the true God Who knows the names of His own.

13. The task Jesus assigned to Mary Magdalene was one of
    honor as He specifically gave to her the privilege of testify-
    ing of His resurrection and telling others about Him. His
    instructions continue today, as each believer can obey His
    Word, the Bible. In what ways are you carrying out the task
    (given to all believers, Matthew 28:18–20) to witness to
    others of the work God has done in your life?

Women in Everyday Life
Women Jesus Referenced

PERHAPS YOU HAVE COME to the end of this study and can think of women mentioned in the Gospels that weren't addressed in a previous lesson. To this point, this study has examined each of the women to whom Jesus spoke and with whom He interacted personally. In addition to these, Jesus occasionally spoke of a woman but not directly to her. In other instances, He referred to women in general in terms of daily life and duties.

Personal Recall

1. Can you think of another woman mentioned by Jesus that you haven't yet studied?

Personal Discovery

Some of Jesus' parables and illustrations contain examples with which the women of His day would identify. Read the following Scripture passages and fill in the blanks to complete each sentence.

2. Luke 13:20, 21. When explaining what the kingdom of God is like, Jesus compared it to *leaven* that a woman took and mixed into a large amount of *meal*.

3. Luke 13:34. When mourning over the city of Jerusalem, Jesus likened His desire to protect and care for it to the protective instincts of a mother _hen_ spreading her _wings_ over her brood.

4. Luke 15:8–10. When illustrating God's attitude toward sinners, Jesus told the parable of a woman who _lost_ one of her _silver coins_. When she found it, she rejoiced and shared the good news.

5. Luke 18:1–8. When demonstrating the need to pray and not give up, Jesus told His disciples a parable about a _widow_ who persistently addressed a _judge_ and pleaded with him to grant her _justice_ against her adversary.

In each of the following cases, Jesus commended a woman and portrayed her as industrious and responsible. Read the passage(s), identify the woman and Jesus' commendation, and fill in the blanks to complete each sentence.

6. Mark 12:41–44; Luke 21:1–4. When giving His disciples an example of sacrificial giving, Jesus commended a poor _widow_ who gave a _small_ amount of money, but He valued her gift as a great one because she offered it out of her _heart_. Rather than speaking directly to the woman, Jesus singled her out, drew His disciples' attention to her, and honored her sacrificial act of service.

poverty

7. Matthew 24:19; Mark 13:17. In His Olivet Discourse, Jesus was sympathetic to the condition of _pregnant_ women and _nursing_ mothers who will have to flee when Antichrist demands worship as the world leader during the Tribulation.

8. Matthew 24:41. When Jesus chose an example to depict His future millennial reign, He used an example of _two_ women who will be _grinding_ at the _mill_. One will be taken in judgment for unbelief, and the other will be saved and welcomed by Christ.

9. Matthew 25:1–13. Jesus spoke a parable likening the kingdom of heaven to _ten virgins_ who are encouraged to watch for the appearing of Jesus after the Tribulation.

10. John 16:21. When clarifying His instruction about the future while in the Upper Room, Jesus chose to illustrate grief turning to joy by picturing a woman giving _birth_ and forgetting her _pain_ because of the _joy_ of her _baby_.

11. Matthew 27:55, 56; 28:1–10; Luke 24:1–10; John 19:25. Mary of Cleophas, the mother of the disciple _James_, was another of the named female disciples of Jesus, but none of her words or Jesus' words to her are recorded. She followed Jesus to the end, traveling with Him and caring for His needs. She, too, stood at the foot of the cross. Then she watched His _crucifixion_. She arrived at the empty tomb on Sunday morning, was commissioned to tell the good news to the disciples, and saw the resurrected Jesus. Even without words, it is clear that Jesus accepted the service and support of this woman and nurtured her as one of His followers.

The most striking thing about the interactions Jesus had with women is that they are recorded at all. Recognizing their involvement in the life and teaching of Jesus certainly went against Jewish culture. In his book *Man and Woman in Biblical Perspective,* James Hurley wrote, "Although the gospels do not record any words of Jesus that repudiate the view of the day about women, their uniform testimony to the presence of women among the followers of Jesus and to His serious teaching of them constitutes a break with tradition and culture."[1]

Consider the balance between the opportunities Jesus gave to women as well as to men. Again, read the passage cited and complete the sentence by filling in the blanks.

12. Luke 1:46–55. Both _Mary_ and Zacharias have a song recorded.

13. Luke 2:36–38. Both Simeon and _Anna_ welcomed Jesus in the temple.

14. John 4. Both the _woman at the well_ _____ and Nicodemus had appointments with Jesus during which He talked about how to have everlasting life.

15. John 11:27. Both Simon Peter and _Martha_ affirmed Jesus as the Christ, the Son of the living God.

16. Luke 13:10–17. Both a man and a woman were healed in the _synagogue_

17. Luke 8:1–3. Both men and women were _disciples_ of Jesus who traveled with Him.

We are so privileged! Jesus ministered to women as the One Who gave dignity and value to their abilities to think well as students, worship well as believers, and minister well as servants.

He did this by speaking to them, teaching them, commending them, revealing Himself, and giving opportunity to be changed by Him.

Jesus has given to each of us the duty and privilege of learning of Him, believing in Him, loving Him, serving Him, and witnessing for Him.

Recall some of the messages Jesus communicated to the women we have studied:

- Though submissive to His mother, Jesus told her that the greatest priority of life is to live and act in accord with the will of God.

- He offered the water of life to the woman of Samaria and told her that if she accepted His gift of water, she would never thirst again.

- He communicated to Peter's mother-in-law and her family that intercession is never too small for His attention.

- He showed the widow of Nain that He has compassion for us during times of loss.

- He told the woman who wiped His feet with her hair that it was her faith, rather than her action, that had saved her.

- He accepted the financial support of the women who followed Him, and He allowed them the privilege of supporting His work.
- He restored the woman who had been bleeding for twelve years by addressing her as "Daughter."
- He gave new life to a girl who died, yet He wanted people to focus on His gospel of salvation.
- He responded to the Canaanite woman's request that she offered persistently because of her great faith and humility.
- He communicated hope, instruction, and healing through repentance to the woman caught in adultery.
- He told Martha that He is the resurrection and the life, her only hope for salvation.
- He commended Mary for her extravagant worship and devotion to Him.
- He corrected a woman in a crowd by teaching her that the greatest blessing comes through focus and obedience on His Word.
- He singled out a woman who had been crippled for eighteen years and gave her the freedom that is not available through the Mosaic law.
- He turned Salome's focus from ruling to the greater one: serving.
- He cautioned the daughters of Jerusalem that life for the next generation would be hard.
- He called Mary Magdalene by name and assigned her a task in His service.

Personal Reflection

Think personally—what is it that the Lord wants you to hear? What is your greatest need? Is it to drink of the water of

life? to turn away from your sin and be cleansed through repentance and forgiveness? to be reminded that God's greatest
gift is salvation? to recognize that Jesus is God, the resurrection and the life, and your only hope for salvation?

What is your greatest need? Is it to be submissive to the
purpose God has for your life? to be restored after a period of
weariness and hurt or illness? to be devoted to Jesus Christ
and to worship Him in spirit and in truth? to hear the Word
of God, to ponder and memorize it, and be changed by it? to
be set free from bondage that cripples and hinders service to
the Lord and others? to serve others rather than waiting and
aspiring for their service to you?

What is your greatest need? Is it to cry out to Jesus for
someone you love who is ill? to turn to Jesus during the pain of
a recent loss? to be given hope even though you have failed? to
be involved in representing Jesus to others who are confused,
hurting, and seeking? to appeal persistently to Jesus with an
attitude of humility? to pray for your children and grandchildren and to help them be prepared for trials that will come to
them? to demonstrate your faith in Jesus Christ by showing it
to others? to be assigned a task for the service of the Lord?

18. Which of the messages Jesus communicated do you want
    to be certain to remember?

19. Write out a verse of Scripture from the account of that in-
    teraction between Jesus and a woman/women. Memorize
    it and meditate on (think about) it.

Endnote

1 James Hurley, *Man and Woman in Biblical Perspective* (Grand Rapids: Zonder-
   van, 1981), 82.

Leader's Guide

Suggestions for Leaders

The effectiveness of a group Bible study usually depends on the leader and the ladies' commitment to prepare beforehand and interact during the study. You cannot totally control the second factor, but you have total control over the first one. These brief suggestions will help you be an effective Bible study leader.

Prepare each lesson a week in advance. During the week, read supplemental material and look for illustrations in the everyday events of your life and in the lives of others.

Encourage the ladies to complete each lesson before the meeting itself. This preparation will make the discussion more interesting.

The physical setting in which you meet will have some bearing on the study itself. Choose an informal setting that will encourage women to relax and participate. In addition to an informal setting, create an atmosphere in which ladies feel free to participate and be themselves.

During the discussion time, here are a few things to observe.

- Don't do all the talking. This study is not designed to be a lecture.
- Encourage discussion on each question by adding ideas and questions. Some are suggested in the Answers section.
- Don't discuss controversial issues that will divide the group. (Differences of opinion are healthy; divisions are not.)
- Don't allow one lady to dominate the discussion. Use statements such as these to draw others into the study: "Let's hear from someone on this side of the room" (the side opposite the dominant talker); "Let's hear from someone who has not shared yet today."
- Stay on the subject. The tendency toward tangents is always possible in a discussion. One of your responsibilities as the leader is to keep the group on track.
- Don't get bogged down on a question that interests only one person.
- When there is no right or wrong answer to a question, the answer key says, "Personal answers." This doesn't mean that the question cannot be answered aloud, just that the question will be answered from a personal perspective. Feel free to invite ladies to respond aloud if they desire. But keep in mind the points listed above to keep your discussion uplifting and on track.

You may want to use the last fifteen minutes of the scheduled time for prayer. If you have a large group of ladies, divide into smaller groups for prayer. You could call this the "Share and Care Time."

If you have a morning Bible study, encourage the ladies to go out for lunch with someone else from time to time. This is a good way to get acquainted with new ladies. Occasionally you could plan a time when ladies bring their own lunches or salads to share and eat together. These things help promote fellowship and friendship in the group.

The formats that follow are suggestions only. You can plan your own format, use one of these, or adapt one of these to your needs.

2-hour Bible Study

10:00—10:15	Coffee and fellowship time
10:15—10:30	Get-acquainted time
	Have two ladies take five minutes each to tell something about themselves and their families.
	Also use this time to make announcements and, if appropriate, take an offering for the babysitters.
10:30—11:45	Bible study
	Leader guides discussion of the questions in the day's lesson.
11:45—12:00	Prayer time

2-hour Bible Study

10:00—10:45	Bible lesson
	Leader teaches a lesson on the content of the material. No discussion during this time.
10:45—11:00	Coffee and fellowship
11:00—11:45	Discussion time
	Divide into small groups with an appointed leader for each group. Discuss the questions in the day's lesson.
11:45—12:00	Prayer time

1½-hour Bible Study

10:00—10:30	Bible study
	Leader guides discussion of half the questions in the day's lesson.
10:30—10:45	Coffee and fellowship
10:45—11:15	Bible study
	Leader continues discussion of the questions in the day's lesson.
11:15—11:30	Prayer time

Answers

LESSON 1

1. Personal answers.
2. Personal answers.
3. Personal answers.
4.

Passage	Person Addressed	Jesus' Words
Luke 2:41–50	His mother, Mary	Why did you seek Me? Did you not know that I must be about My Father's business?
John 2:1–11	His mother, Mary	Woman, what does your concern have to do with Me? My hour has not yet come.
John 19:26, 27	His mother, Mary	Woman, behold your son!
John 4:5–42	The Samaritan woman Jesus met at a well	Give Me a drink. If you knew the gift of God, and who it is who says to you, "Give Me a drink," you would have asked Him, and He would have given you living water. Whoever drinks of this water will thirst again, 14 but whoever drinks of the water that I shall give him will never thirst. But the water that I shall give him will become in him a fountain of water springing up into everlasting life. Go, call your husband, and come here. You have well said, "I have no husband," or you have had five husbands, and the one whom you now have is not your husband; in that you spoke truly. Woman, believe Me, the hour is coming when you will neither on this mountain, nor in Jerusalem, worship the Father. You worship what you do not know; we know what we worship, for salvation is of the Jews. But the hour is coming, and now is, when the true worshipers will worship the Father in spirit and truth; for the Father is seeking such to worship Him. God is Spirit, and those who worship Him must worship in spirit and truth. I who speak to you am He.
Matthew 8:14, 15; Mark 1:29–31; Luke 4:38, 39	Peter's mother-in-law	*The Bible does not record anything said directly to her.*
Luke 7:11–17	A widow from Nain whose son had died	Do not weep.

Passage	Person Addressed	Jesus' Words
Luke 7:36–50	A woman with the reputation of a sinner	Your sins are forgiven. Your faith has saved you. Go in peace.
Matthew 27:55, 56; Mark 15:40, 41; Luke 8:1–3; 23:49	Mary Magdalene, Mary the mother of James and Joses, Salome, Joanna, Susanna, and the mother of James and John	*The Bible does not record anything He said specifically to them, except to the mother of James and John (see below) and to them as a group (see below).*
Matthew 9:20–22; Mark 5:26–34; Luke 8:43–48	A woman who had been bleeding for twelve years	Who touched My clothes? Daughter, your faith has made you well. Go in peace, and be healed of your affliction. Daughter, be of good cheer; your faith has made you well. Go in peace.
Matthew 9:18, 19, 23–26; Mark 5:21–24, 35–43; Luke 8:41, 42, 49–56	Jairus' daughter	Talitha, cumi, which is translated, Little girl, I say to you, arise. Little girl, arise.
Matthew 15:21–28; Mark 7:24–30	A Gentile woman with a demon-possessed daughter	It is not good to take the children's bread and throw it to the little dogs. O woman, great is your faith! Let it be to you as you desire. Let the children be filled first, for it is not good to take the children's bread and throw it to the little dogs. And she answered and said to Him, "Yes, Lord, yet even the little dogs under the table eat from the children's crumbs." Then He said to her, "For this saying go your way; the demon has gone out of your daughter."
John 8:1–11	A Jewish woman caught in adultery	Woman, where are those accusers of yours? Has no one condemned you? Jesus said to her, Neither do I condemn you; go and sin no more.
Luke 10:38–42	Martha	Martha, Martha, you are worried and troubled about many things. But one thing is needed, and Mary has chosen that good part, which will not be taken away from her.
John 11:1–44	Martha	Your brother will rise again. I am the resurrection and the life. He who believes in Me, though he may die, he shall live. And whoever lives and believes in Me shall never die. Do you believe this?

Passage	Person Addressed	Jesus' Words
John 11:1–44	Mary	Where have you laid him?
Matthew 26:6–13; Mark 14:3–9; John 12:2–8	She is unnamed	*He spoke over her, not to her.* Let her alone; she has kept this for the day of My burial. For the poor you have with you always, but Me you do not have always.
Luke 11:27, 28	An anonymous woman in the company of people Jesus was teaching	More than that, blessed are those who hear the word of God and keep it!
Luke 13:10–17	A woman with a crippling physical infirmity	Woman, you are loosed from your infirmity.
Matthew 20:20–23; 27:55, 56	The mother of James and John	What do you wish? You do not know what you ask. Are you able to drink the cup that I am about to drink, and be baptized with the baptism that I am baptized with?
Luke 23:28–31	A group of unidentified women who followed Jesus	Daughters of Jerusalem, do not weep for Me, but weep for yourselves and for your children. For indeed the days are coming in which they will say, "Blessed are the barren, wombs that never bore, and breasts which never nursed!" Then they will begin to say to the mountains, "Fall on us!" and to the hills, "Cover us!" For if they do these things in the green wood, what will be done in the dry?
Luke 8:2	Mary Magdalene	*Nothing Jesus said to her is recorded until after the Resurrection. See below.*
Mark 15:47; 16:9; John 20:11–18	Mary Magdalene	Woman, why are you weeping? Mary! Do not cling to Me, for I have not yet ascended to My Father; but go to My brethren and say to them, "I am ascending to My Father and your Father, and to My God and your God."

LESSON 2

1. Possible answers: As a perpetual virgin; as a sinless woman; as one to be worshiped; as an intercessor in prayers to her Son on our behalf; as a woman who was not capable of sin; as a woman who can save people from their sins.
2. Personal answers.
3. (a) She lived in Nazareth in Galilee. She was a virgin. She was engaged to Joseph. (b) He addressed her as the highly favored one.

4. That she was highly favored and blessed; the Lord was with her; she should not be afraid; and she had found favor with God.

5. His name would be Jesus. He would be great and the Son of the Highest. God would give Him the throne of David, from which her Son would rule over Israel forever.

6. Paraphrases may vary.

7. The Holy Spirit would come upon Mary; God's power would overshadow her; her child would be the Son of God.

8. Her cousin Elizabeth, though old, was six months pregnant.

9. (a) "Blessed are you among women, and blessed is the fruit of your womb!" (b) Possible answers: She was a godly woman, for the Holy Spirit had come upon her. He told her that Mary was bearing the Son of God. She spoke God-breathed (inspired) words. Even the yet-unborn John was moved by the Holy Spirit to respond to Mary's voice. Elizabeth knew that Mary carried her Savior, implying her need for a Savior.

10. She called God her Savior. She said He had regarded her low estate, or humble state. Neither of her statements lend themselves to the erroneous belief that she is a co-redeemer and mediator with Jesus Christ.

11. That her Son would be opposed; that she would be hurt as if a sword pierced her soul; that the many who believed in Him would "rise," while those who did not would "fall."

12. Possible answers: She had to carry the shame of apparently but not really being immoral. Many may have thought her Son was a bastard. She had to leave her home for Bethlehem and then Bethlehem for Egypt. Settling in back home after being gone may have brought sorrow as she learned of the passing of loved ones. The children she had with Joseph did not at first receive Jesus as their Messiah; they thought He was crazy. She watched her Son opposed through rejection, hatred, and crucifixion. She loved Him and watched His death, knowing He was not guilty. Even though He rose again, He did not stay with her; in a sense, she lost Him again.

13. (a) In the temple. (b) Asking questions and listening to the answers of the Jewish scholars there.

14. Possible answers: Jesus chose this crucial stage in His life, when He was on the brink of manhood, to tell Mary and Joseph in an unforgettable way that He knew the identity of His real Father and what that would mean for His mission. Jesus recognized His unique relationship to God and knew that His mission would require a devotion to God's purposes so great that it would take precedence over family ties. He knew He would follow His mission, even at the cost of pain and misunderstanding.

15. She believed that Jesus could take care of the problem, that He was able to meet needs. She believed in His authority over everything and everyone, and she communicated submission.

16. Seeing her innocent Son die for others' wrongdoing, including her own, must have felt like a sword piercing her soul (Luke 2:35).

LESSON 3

1. Personal answers.

2. Personal answers. (Keep these answers private.)
3. She had been married five times and was not married to the man with whom she was currently living. Her reputation was such that the men of the city came out to see Jesus based on her testimony. There were only two people at the well, which indicates that the woman didn't go when the other women did.
4. Possible answers: It was Jesus who initiated the conversation, and He did so by making a request. Jesus used water, a very common element, as the basis of the conversation. He did not give direct answers to her questions. Jesus did not debate with the woman when she tried to change the subject. He addressed the greatest need in her life.
5. He asked her to do Him a favor—draw water. He asked questions, and segued into telling her about eternal life. He revealed her sinfulness. He offered her a better way—to worship "in spirit and truth."
6. Forgiveness of sin and peace with God.
7. It provides continual satisfaction; anyone who drinks it will have within him- or herself a spring of living water.
8. Get your husband.
9. She realized that He was no ordinary man and might even be a prophet. She changed the subject to focus on the place of worship.
10. True worship is in spirit and truth, which is more important than the place.
11. She admitted her sin. She told people what Jesus had done. She brought people to Jesus.

LESSON 4

1. Personal answers.
2. (a) She was at Peter's house. She was in bed, suffering with a fever. Jesus rebuked the fever. Jesus touched her hand, and the fever left. She immediately waited on those in the house, which included Jesus, Simon, Andrew, James, and John. (b) Luke alone notes that people asked Jesus to heal Peter's mother-in-law.
3. Possible answers: Did she live there all the time? What were her and her daughter's names? What had made her ill? How long had she been ill?
4. She immediately served them, which would require good health and energy.
5. Personal answers.
6. Personal answers.
7. Personal answers.
8. Personal answers.
9. Personal answers.
10. She was a widow. She had no husband with whom to walk through her trial and loss.
11. (a) Do not weep. (b) He told the man to arise.
12. As making Him unclean.

LESSON 5

1. Personal answers.
2. Personal answers.

3. As a sinner.
4. She stood weeping; she was ready when Jesus came; she was prepared for her worship of Him. Her actions conveyed belief that He was the Messiah. She demonstrated her love for Jesus by washing, kissing, and anointing His feet.
5. She washed Jesus' feet with tears, and wiped them with the hairs of her head, while Simon did not wash them at all. She kissed His feet, while Simon had not kissed Him at all. She anointed Jesus' feet with ointment, while Simon failed to anoint Jesus' head.
6. "Your sins are forgiven" (v. 48) and "Your faith has saved you. Go in peace" (v. 50).
7. Personal answers.
8. Personal answers.
9. Personal answers.
10. *Mary Magdalene*—Seven demons had been cast out of her. *Joanna*—She was married to the steward of King Herod.
11. Possible answer: They can come from any background and station of life.
12. (a) Women with a dark past (e.g., mental illness, substance abuse, involvement in a cult, victim of sex trafficking, victim of other abuse). (b) Women in politics or married to a politician; women who work for the federal government or whose husbands do. (c) Personal answers.
13.

Woman's Name	Individual Identification
Mary Magdalene	She was at Jesus' crucifixion. She had followed Jesus in Galilee and up to Jerusalem.
Mary	She was the mother of James and Joses. She had followed Jesus in Galilee and up to Jerusalem.
Unnamed woman, presumed to be Salome	She was the wife of Zebedee and mother of James and John.
Joanna	She was married to Chuza, Herod's steward.

LESSON 6

1. Personal answers.
2. Personal answers.
3. It was hopeless.
4. She was desperate.
5. She had had the problem for twelve years; doctors couldn't heal her; her disease was getting worse; she had run out of money.
6. Her bed, anything she sat on, and anyone who touched her bed or seat.
7. For practical purposes, people would want to separate themselves from her. Because all who touched her would be at risk, others would not have entered her home or invited her to be in theirs. She could not worship with others in the synagogue.
8. It was great, for she thought, "I will be healed," not "I might be healed."
9. It would not reappear.

10. Who touched My clothes?
11. Fearing and trembling, she knelt before Jesus.
12. She told Him the entire truth. She told Him why she had touched Him as well as what had happened to her.
13. "Daughter, your faith has made you well. Go in peace, and be healed of your affliction."

LESSON 7
1. Personal answers.
2. Personal answers.
3. (a) A ruler in a synagogue. (b) For Jesus to heal his daughter.
4. "Worshiped him" and "he fell at His feet and begged Him earnestly."
5. Someone from the ruler's house came with the message that Jairus' daughter had died.
6. "Do not be afraid; only believe."
7. (a) Peter, James, John, and the girl's parents. (b) Why are you making such an ado and weeping? The girl is only sleeping.
8. He took her hand and said, "I say to you, arise."
9. Personal answers.

LESSON 8
1. Personal answers.
2. Trying to find seclusion in a friend's house.
3. To cast a demon out of her daughter (v. 26). To get a crumb of God's blessing on the Jews (v. 28).
4. (a) He remained silent. (b) "It is not good to take the children's bread and throw it to the little dogs."
5. She agreed and asked for "crumbs."
6. The mother's faith.
7. Personal answers.
8. Personal answers.
9. Possible answers: hopelessness, betrayal, fear.
10. The law against adultery, for which the penalty was death.
11. To test and accuse Jesus.
12. He would be put to death too.
13. "He who is without sin among you, let him throw a stone at her first."
14. Where are your accusers? Is anyone condemning you?
15. "No one, Lord."
16. I don't condemn you; go and do not sin anymore.
17. Personal answers.

LESSON 9
1. Personal answers.
2. Personal answers.
3. Personal answers.
4. Personal answers.

5. Personal answers.
6. For pursuing things other than the one "needed" thing.
7. That Jesus cared more about relationship than about actions/serving.
8. "But one thing is needed, and Mary has chosen that good part, which will not be taken away from her."
9. Personal answers.
10. Jesus loved Lazarus.
11. Personal answers.
12. Raised Lazarus from the dead.
13. They thought the perfume could have had a more practical use.
14. He defended Mary.
15. That Jesus would die and be buried.

LESSON 10
1. Personal answers.
2. Personal answers.
3. Jesus was speaking truth about Himself: that His power came from God, not Satan; that those who are not with Him are against Him. He also spoke about Satan: that he doesn't divide demon against demon; that a demon might leave a person but it would come back, bringing other demons with it.
4. Blessed (happy) is the woman who bore and nursed Jesus.
5. Those who hear and keep God's words are blessed ones.
6. Personal answers.
7. Personal answers.
8. Personal answers.
9. Personal answers.
10. As one who followed Jesus and ministered to Him.
11. That her sons, James and John, could sit on either side of Jesus' throne in His kingdom.
12. She kneeled before Jesus and asked regarding His future kingdom; this indicates she believed in Him as Messiah.
13. He said that she did not know what she was asking. He asked James and John if they were able to drink from His cup or be baptized (with suffering, pain, and grief) as He would be.
14. God the Father.
15. She continued to follow Him and care for and about Him.

LESSON 11
1. Personal answers.
2. "Spirit of infirmity" rather than "infirmity" or a more specific name (Luke 13:11); "loosed from this bond" (v. 16).
3. In a synagogue on the Sabbath.
4. "Woman, you are loosed from your infirmity."
5. No.
6. She glorified God.
7. Jesus healed on the Sabbath. The ruler of the synagogue saw this as work on

the Sabbath. He was locked into religious adherence to the Mosaic law and Jewish tradition. The letter of the law and traditions were more important to him than the spirit and intent of the law.

8. He addressed the crowd and asked whether they (including the woman) had six days in which to work or, by implication, be healed.

9. Personal answers.

10. Jesus called the ruler a hypocrite and asked if a woman shouldn't be treated better than the law allowed an animal to be treated.

11. (a) "Daughter of Abraham." (b) As a Jew, the woman was one of God's Chosen People, precious in His sight.

12. Personal answers.

13. Personal answers.

14. Weep for yourselves and your children, not for Me.

LESSON 12

1. Personal answers.

2. She was possessed by seven demons and under Satan's influence.

3. Possible answer: Since she was possessed, she was tortured—most likely with destruction, pain, torment, and suffering; she was desperate and seemingly incurable.

4. *Ephesians 6:10–20*—We are to be strong in the Lord's power, not our own; we are to put on the whole armor of God, which will allow us to stand against the wiles of the Devil. *1 Peter 5:8, 9*—Be sober (cool; marked by calm reasonableness and free from purely emotional appeal), be vigilant (watchful) because the Devil looks for those he can devour. Resist him by being steadfast in the faith. Know that you are not alone.

5. Mary Magdalene was at the cross, watching all that happened.

6. She watched to see where Jesus was buried; she returned to the burial site after the Sabbath so she could anoint His body with spices. She wanted to minister to Him even after His death.

7. (a) An angel. (b) Deliver the news of Jesus' resurrection to the (male) disciples and tell them where Jesus would meet them (in Galilee, Matt. 28:7).

8. (a) She initially thought that the risen Jesus was the gardener. (b) When He said her name.

9. To tell His brethren (followers) that He was going to ascend to His Father and their Father, to His God and to their God. (She was privileged to be the first to see Jesus alive.) Then He gave her the license and authority to be the first to testify of His resurrection.

LESSON 13

1. Personal answers.

2. When explaining what the kingdom of God is like, Jesus compared it to *leaven* that a woman took and mixed into a large amount of *meal*.

3. When mourning over the city of Jerusalem, Jesus likened His desire to protect and care for it to the protective instincts of a mother *hen* spreading her *wings* over her brood.

4. When illustrating God's attitude toward sinners, Jesus told the parable of a woman who *lost* one of her *silver pieces*. When she found it, she rejoiced and shared the good news.

5. When demonstrating the need to pray and not give up, Jesus told His disciples a parable about a *widow* who persistently addressed a *judge* and pleaded with him to grant her *justice* against her adversary.

6. When giving His disciples an example of sacrificial giving, Jesus commended a poor *widow* who gave a *small* amount of money, but He valued her gift as a great one because she offered it out of her *poverty*. Rather than speaking directly to the woman, Jesus singled her out, drew His disciples' attention to her, and honored her sacrificial act of service.

7. In His Olivet Discourse, Jesus was sympathetic to the condition of *pregnant* women and *nursing* mothers who will have to flee when Antichrist demands worship as the world leader during the Tribulation.

8. When Jesus chose an example to depict His future millennial reign, He used an example of *two* women who will be *grinding* at the *mill*. One will be taken in judgment for unbelief, and the other, a believer, will be left on earth in her physical body to inhabit the millennial Kingdom, ruled by Christ.

9. Jesus spoke a parable likening the kingdom of heaven to *ten virgins* who are encouraged to watch for the appearing of the bridegroom (Jesus) (after the Tribulation).

10. When clarifying His instruction about the future while in the Upper Room, Jesus chose to illustrate grief turning to joy by picturing a woman giving *birth* and forgetting her anguish because of the *joy* of her *baby*.

11. Mary of Cleophas, the mother of the disciple *James*, was another of the named female disciples of *Jesus*, but none of her words or Jesus' words to her are recorded. She followed Jesus to the end, traveling with Him and caring for His needs. She, too, stood at the foot of the cross. Then she watched His *death*. She arrived at the empty tomb on Sunday morning, was commissioned to tell the good news to the disciples, and saw the resurrected Jesus. Even without words, it is clear that Jesus accepted the service and support of this woman and nurtured her as one of His followers.

12. Both *Mary* and Zacharias have a song recorded.

13. Both Simeon and *Anna* welcomed Jesus in the temple.

14. Both the *woman at the well* and Nicodemus had appointments with Jesus during which He talked about how to have everlasting life.

15. Both Simon Peter and *Martha* affirmed Jesus as the Christ, the Son of the living God.

16. Both a man and a woman were healed in the *synagogue*.

17. Both men and women were *disciples* of Jesus who traveled with Him.

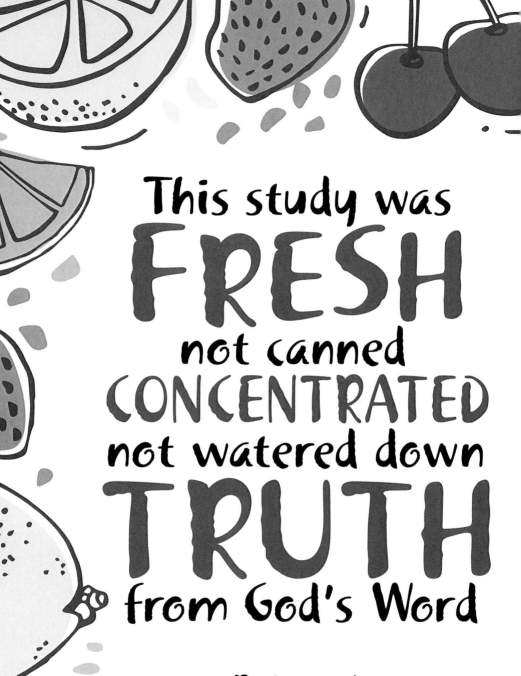

This study was
FRESH
not canned
CONCENTRATED
not watered down
TRUTH
from God's Word

Pick another at
RBPstore.org/women

Women Who Met the Master

From His birth to His death, the Lord Jesus Christ interacted with women. He loved, taught, respected, empowered, forgave, and healed them. He learned from them, received their worship, accepted their support, and generally lifted their position in society. These 13 lessons move from the typical "women of the Bible" study to focus on Jesus' own personal interactions with women of His day. In this study, you'll learn to appreciate and love the Lord Jesus even more. Your life will change as you interact with Jesus!

ABOUT THE AUTHOR

Carolyn Culver serves with her husband, David, in church, missions, and writing ministries. As a former pastor's wife, she has worked closely with Christian families for three decades. In addition to writing three books with David (*Family Life, Marriage,* and *Parenting*), Carolyn has written *Protected by God's Providence,* a women's Bible study on Esther. Carolyn and David have four adult children and several grandchildren.

ISBN-13: 978-1-62940-611-4

9 781629 406114

RBP5168

RegularBaptistPress.org
Building Lives By the Book

RBP